Wordsworth's Experiments with Tradition

The Lyric Poems of 1802

Wordsworth's Experiments with Tradition

The Lyric Poems of 1802

WITH TEXTS OF THE POEMS
BASED ON EARLY MANUSCRIPTS

JARED R. CURTIS

CORNELL UNIVERSITY PRESS

ITHACA AND LONDON

Copyright © 1971 by Cornell University

First published 1971 by Cornell University Press.
Published in the United Kingdom by Cornell University Press Ltd.,
2-4 Brook Street, London W1Y 1AA.

International Standard Book Number 0-8014-0662-5
Library of Congress Catalog Card Number 78-162546

PRINTED IN THE UNITED STATES OF AMERICA
BY VAIL-BALLOU PRESS, INC.

For Ida

Preface

In no comparably brief period of his life did William Wordsworth write a greater variety of memorable poems than in the spring and early summer of 1802. In making these experiments with tradition, he reached a significant turn in his poetic development. The purpose of this study is to examine this group of some thirty poems in a series of essays that move from general to more and more specific concerns. The essays describe and analyze the human context of the poems of 1802, the poet's emerging sense of purpose in composing them, and his experiments in form, language, and the craft of poetry. Finally, the last two chapters examine the two poems generally regarded as among the highest achievements of the poet and as central texts in the development of his mind and art. "Resolution and Independence," surviving in two quite different versions, is an apt illustration of the poet's artistic development during the early months of 1802. The "Immortality Ode," though in part composed after 1802, reveals a design that depends both on the lyric voice that Wordsworth learned to use in the poetry of 1802 and on the steadier, more somber voice of the later Wordsworth, the voice of the "humaniz'd" soul.

In order to set my remarks on these poems in a larger critical context, I have included a brief bibliographical note at the end of each chapter. The poems themselves appear at the end of the book in the order of their composition. They have been edited to achieve as nearly as possible their form in 1802, when they were first "finished."

It is pleasant to acknowledge here the many debts incurred in the preparation of this book. Grants from the Danforth Foundation, The National Endowment for the Humanities, and the Research and Advanced Studies program at Indiana University have given me the needed time for research and writing. The encouragement and guidance of the late John A. Finch and of Ephim G. Fogel, Stephen M. Parrish, and Geoffrey H. Hartman were of immense help in the early stages of research. Kenneth R. Johnston and Russell Noyes read the manuscript with patience and skill. Boyd M. Berry, David Bleich, Stuart M. Sperry, Jr., and Owen Thomas asked diverse but difficult and penetrating questions about Chapters 6 and 7. Mark L. Reed and Jonathan Wordsworth have saved me from error more times than I care to enumerate. To George H. Healey, Curator of Rare Books for the Cornell University Libraries, I am especially grateful for his steady and kindly encouragement, first and last. The sixth chapter, on "Resolution and Independence," first printed in the *Cornell Library Journal* (Spring 1970), has been revised and appears here with the permission of the editor. Chapters 1 and 2, in briefer form, were given as a lecture at The Rydal Mount Summer School, July 1971. In the introduction to the texts I have acknowledged my indebtedness to libraries for the use of Wordsworth materials, but I am particularly grateful to the Trustees of Dove Cottage for permission to use the rich resources of the Wordsworth Library at Grasmere.

J. R. C.

Simon Fraser University

Contents

Abbreviations

BL	S. T. Coleridge. *Biographia Literaria*, ed. J. Shawcross. 2 vols. Oxford: Clarendon Press, 1907, rpt. 1967.
C.	Samuel Taylor Coleridge
DC; DCP	Dove Cottage; Dove Cottage Papers
D. W.	Dorothy Wordsworth
DWJ	*The Journals of Dorothy Wordsworth*, ed. Helen Darbishire. Oxford: Oxford Univ. Press, 1958.
EY	*The Letters of William and Dorothy Wordsworth: The Early Years, 1787–1805*, ed. Ernest de Selincourt. 2d ed., rev. Chester L. Shaver. Oxford: Clarendon Press, 1967.
IF notes	Notes dictated to Isabella Fenwick by Wordsworth.
LCW	*Literary Criticism of Wordsworth*, ed. Paul M. Zall. Lincoln, Neb.: Univ. of Nebraska Press, 1966.
L	Longman MS of *Poems* (1807), British Museum.
LY	*The Letters of William and Dorothy Wordsworth: The Later Years, 1821–1850*, ed. Ernest de Selincourt. 3 vols. Oxford: Clarendon Press, 1939. (Cited as *LY* 1, 2, or 3.)
M	Dove Cottage MS Verse 25 (MS M of *Prel*).

M. H., M. W.	Mary Hutchinson Wordsworth
Moorman 1	Mary Moorman. *William Wordsworth, a Biography: The Early Years, 1770–1803.* Oxford: Clarendon Press, 1957. Reprinted from corrected sheets, 1965.
Moorman 2	Mary Moorman. *William Wordsworth, a Biography: The Later Years, 1803–1850.* Oxford: Clarendon Press, 1965.
MY	*The Letters of William and Dorothy Wordsworth: The Middle Years,* ed. Ernest de Selincourt. 2d ed., rev. Mary Moorman and Alan G. Hill. 2 vols. Oxford: Clarendon Press, 1969–1970. (Cited as *MY* 2 or 3.)
Poems (1807)	William Wordsworth, *Poems in Two Volumes.* London: Longman, Hurst, Rees, and Orme, 1807. (In the notes to the text, simply 1807.)
Prel	*The Prelude,* ed. Ernest de Selincourt, rev. Helen Darbishire. Oxford: Clarendon Press, 1959. (Unless otherwise noted, the 1805 text is the one cited.)
PW	*The Poetical Works of William Wordsworth,* ed. Ernest de Selincourt, rev. Helen Darbishire. 5 vols. Oxford: Clarendon Press, 1940–1949. Vols. 1 and 2 rev. 1952.
R. W.	Richard Wordsworth
S. H.	Sara Hutchinson
SHP	"Sara Hutchinson's Poets" (a notebook of 1802 and after kept by the poet's sister-in-law; in DCP, uncatalogued).
STCL	*Collected Letters of Samuel Taylor Coleridge,* ed. E. L. Griggs. 4 vols. to date. Oxford: Clarendon Press, 1956——.
STCNB	*The Notebooks of Samuel Taylor Coleridge,* ed. Kathleen Coburn. 2 vols. to date. Princeton, N.J.: Princeton Univ. Press, 1957——.
W.	William Wordsworth

[PART I]

EXPERIMENTS
WITH TRADITION

[1]
Wordsworth in 1802:
The Poetry of Crisis

Most students of Wordsworth have recognized the spring
of 1802 as a crucial stage in the poet's life, one in which an
expanding and many-sided crisis took shape. He had much
on his mind. Among the most pressing matters were the
legal struggles over Lord Lonsdale's debt to Wordsworth's
father and the economic pinch felt as a consequence of the
long refusal to pay that debt. Wordsworth's plans for marriage with Mary Hutchinson were fraught not only with
economic difficulties but with social and emotional ones as
well. He and his sister Dorothy had to readjust to make a
family of three, while at the same time moving to exclude
that other family, Annette Vallon and Wordsworth's illegiti-
mate daughter. The strain of this painful and complicated
issue is too often glossed over. Wordsworth's original plans
were to marry in the spring. The negotiations preparatory to
the treaty of Amiens allowed correspondence with Annette
again, after ten years of separation and perhaps two years of
silence, and led finally, with the signing of the treaty, to the
poet's making some kind of settlement with Annette and
their daughter, Caroline, in France, August 1802. The
decision to go was made on March 22: "We resolved to see

Annette," Dorothy writes in her journal.[1] But the decision also meant postponing the wedding until after the trip had been made and the settlement arranged. There is no question that Wordsworth looked forward to a happy marriage with Mary Hutchinson; but his anxiety over the unresolved ties with Annette and his concern for the states of mind of Mary and Dorothy temper the picture of a happy Wordsworth so often drawn.[2]

Coleridge's unhappy marriage, his love for Sara Hutchinson, his ill health, and his deepening "dejection" must be taken into account as having a profound effect upon Wordsworth. Furthermore, Wordsworth had his own fears over the loss of his poetic powers, principally in that special Wordsworthian faculty, his memory, until recently a rich and unfailing resource, but now waning, he seemed to feel. He saw persuasive signs that the fallow period of rest and poetic silence was lengthening, while the creative time, for which it had always been a preparation, shrank. The evidence of letters, journals, and manuscripts suggests that Wordsworth did most of his composing during the winter and spring months, resting and travelling during the summer and fall. Dorothy, a close observer of her brother's ways, has recorded her awareness of the cyclical nature of his inspiration. In a letter to Lady Beaumont in 1805 she looks for-

[1] STCL, 2:788; EY, 1:282; DWJ, 137, 138. The treaty was signed on March 26, 1802, thus making travel between the two countries again possible.

[2] Albert S. Gérard has suggested that Wordsworth had "his own secret misgivings about the possibility of reconciling his devotion to his future wife and his dedication to poetry" (English Romantic Poets [Berkeley and Los Angeles, 1968], p. 127). Dorothy Wordsworth's uneasiness is apparent from her journal (for example, DWJ, 141 [April 13, 14]). Wordsworth visited Mary twice that spring, once before the decision to postpone the wedding, perhaps to tell her of his ties with

ward to "winter quiet and loneliness" when "starlight walks and winter winds are his delight—his mind I think is often more fertile in this season than any other."[3] The years 1796 to 1799 followed this pattern of creativity. But late 1800 and all of 1801 were poetically barren times, productive of only a few poems and translations. The poet's problems, then, ranging in nature from practical but important concerns to a crisis of the imagination, pressed in upon him. Wordsworth might be said to have been forced during this time to turn from the hard-pressed souls he depicted in *Lyrical Ballads*—female vagrant, convict, mad mother, forsaken Indian woman—and to face instead his own beleaguered spirit.

The miracle is that, despite or because of the many pressures upon him, Wordsworth began composing again during the late winter and spring of 1802, starting with types of verse familiar to him but reaching out for different forms, creating new ones and experimenting with older ones, though adding as always his own peculiar stamp. Only the brilliantly productive winters, 1798–1799 and 1804–1805, when work on *The Prelude* was most intense, can vie with the late winter and spring of 1802 in the amount and high quality of the verse composed.

The viability of the lyric form became a part of a dialogue between Wordsworth and Coleridge, as they weighed the merits of the long poem and the short lyric. Coleridge's grand scheme for Wordsworth's philosophical poem, *The Recluse*, is well known, as is his persistence in urging Wordsworth to get on with it, even at the expense of other literary

---

Annette (*DWJ*, 119–120 [February, 14–16]), and once afterward (*DWJ*, 140–141 [April 7–13]), to inform her of the decision and perhaps to ease her anxieties.

[3] *EY*, 1:650 (29 November 1805); Moorman, 2:65.

plans or activity. After a plea for the long poem, in a letter written in the fall of 1799, Coleridge adds, "In my present mood, I am wholly against the publication of any small poems." By exploring the connection between Wordsworth's own distinctive short poems and the long philosophical poem planned between the two poets, I hope to define Wordsworth's attitudes toward the lyrics and begin to reveal the characteristic voice in which he wrote them.

Throughout the months of creative activity in the spring of 1802 Coleridge received or heard nearly all the poems that Wordsworth composed. He often liked them, as evidenced by his letter to Thomas Poole in May 1802, where he names and transcribes "2 pleasing little poems of Wordsworth's": "To a Butterfly" and "The Sparrow's Nest." [4] But again in July 1802, Coleridge writes to Southey, after Wordsworth's revised Preface and Appendix on poetic diction had appeared with the third edition of the *Lyrical Ballads,* that "altho' Wordsworth's Preface is half a child of my own Brain . . . yet I am far from going all lengths with [him]." For Wordsworth's defense of his own short poems was beginning to look less and less convincing to Coleridge. He remarks not so much on the number as on the length of the the poems Wordsworth was writing: "a number of Poems (32 in all) some of them of considerable Length (the longest 160 Lines)." Yet all is not well; despite Coleridge's generous allowance that "the greater number of these" are to his "feelings very excellent Compositions," he finds "here & there a daring Humbleness of Language & Versification, and a strict adherence to matter of fact even to prolixity" that "startles" him.[5] The short poems seem inevitably, from Cole-

[4] For this letter and the 1799 letter quoted above see *STCL,* 1:527; 2:800–801.

[5] *STCL,* 2:830. The August 1803 version of "Resolution and Inde-

ridge's point of view, to focus on the literal, to encourage, as he later wrote, "a laborious minuteness and fidelity in the representation of objects, and their positions" which led Wordsworth to "*a biographical attention* to probability, and an *anxiety* of exploration and retrospect." They seem clearly not to prepare him for "what he is capable of producing . . . the FIRST GENUINE PHILOSOPHIC POEM." [6] Over a year after his remarks to Southey, as his relations with Wordsworth became more and more strained, Coleridge again reports to Poole that he regrets Wordsworth's neglect of him, and that he is made to "tremble" at Wordsworth's "Self-involution," his living wholly among "*Devotees,*" his hypochondria, and his dependence upon wife and sister, "lest a Film should rise, and thicken on his moral Eye." But Coleridge finds a basis for his irritation with Wordsworth and a cause for Wordsworth's own "Self-involution" in "the habit . . . of writing such a multitude of small Poems" which has been "hurtful to him." Coleridge finds just cause to rejoice "with a deep & true Joy," that Wordsworth has "at length yielded" to Coleridge's "urgent & repeated—almost unremitting—requests & remonstrances—& will go on with the Recluse exclusively." Then in a characteristically elaborate image Coleridge sums up this apparent turning point in his friend's poetic career by describing *The Recluse* as "a Great Work, in which he will sail; on an open Ocean, & a steady wind; unfretted by short tacks, reefing, & hawling & disentangling the ropes." It is almost as if Wordsworth were the Ancient Mariner himself, at last free of the bewildering and entangling motions of the erratic winds, and on his way home to tell

---

pendence" came to 154 lines. Wordsworth wrote more than thirty-two poems, but not all have been identified. Doubtless some have not survived.

[6] *BL,* 2:103, 129.

his tale. The mythic figure of the poet is set free by his own vision, by his focusing "his attention & Feelings within the circle of great objects & elevated Conceptions." Here is "his natural Element," says Coleridge; "the having been out of it has been his Disease—to return to it is the specific Remedy, both Remedy & Health." Finally, he shifts the metaphoric antitheses from sea-wanderings and the return home, disease and health, to the more appropriately Wordsworthian metaphors of mountain freedom versus urban pettiness. He concludes that it is a "misfortune, that Wordsworth ever deserted his former mountain Track to wander in Lanes & allies." [7] The mountain visions of the largely unwritten *Prelude* come to mind, set off against the unflattering and satiric glimpses of undignified and repressive city life both in and out of the *Prelude*.[8] Brilliant even in self-pity, Coleridge knew his friend's strengths. He was often insensitive, though, to Wordsworth's peculiar lyric gifts.

Why was Coleridge so averse to the short lyric? Shortly before writing this last letter Coleridge confided to his notebook how "sincerely glad" he was that Wordsworth "has bidden farewell to all small Poems—& is devoting himself to his great work." Here for the first time he offers an explicit reason for his condemnation of "little poems": in them Wordsworth's "own corrections, coming *of necessity* so often, at the end of every 14, or 20 lines—or whatever the poem might chance to be—wore him out." Coleridge no doubt speaks of the older poet's habits of composition and revision

[7] *STCL*, 2:1013 (14 October 1803). Coleridge adds, "tho' in the event it may prove to have a great Benefit to him": because Wordsworth's "fretting" has taught him what to avoid, or does Coleridge sense the restorative power of the short poems?

[8] Compare especially the poem "Star-gazers," *PW*, 2:219, 220, and Book VII of *The Prelude*.

from the experience of having watched and aided these struggles throughout the Alfoxden and early Grasmere years. His description of the pain it cost Wordsworth to revise is fully corroborated by a repeated complaint, almost a refrain, in Dorothy's journals. One reads there how she and the poet "sate comfortably by the fire till he began to try to alter *The Butterfly,* and tired himself" or how she finds "William very nervous. After he was in bed, [he was] haunted with altering *The Rainbow.*" There are a great many more such instances. Also among the reflections quoted above, Coleridge suggests a second reason for his not liking small poems. He writes, "Difference of opinion with his best friends [Coleridge among them] irritated him & he wrote at times too much with a sectarian Spirit, in a sort of Bravado." What seems to have happened is that Wordsworth, egged on by Coleridge's remonstrances, produced poems meant to serve as justifications, as brave efforts in an idiom scorned by one of his "best friends." [9]

It is tempting to suppose that these latest remarks of Coleridge stem from conversation between the two poets upon Wordsworth's return from Scotland in October 1803. They must have talked about *The Recluse,* a concern uppermost in both their minds. But Wordsworth, aside from brief stints of work on the *Prelude,* had composed nothing but short poems after his return from Germany. He may even have offered an explanation for his inability to get on with the long poem very like the first one Coleridge makes note of. Wordsworth's longer blank verse poems composed before 1802 had also undergone extensive and painstaking revision, particularly "The Ruined Cottage" and the early form of

[9] *STCNB,* 1546 (October 1803); Miss Coburn suggests between 9 October and 14 October 1803 (*DWJ,* 132 [14 March 1802] and 162 [14 May 1802]). See also Moorman, 1:520–521.

The Prelude.[10] But they seem to have been composed in large blocks, while the process of revision was at least initially a matter of connecting and amplifying the parts composed. Both these poems were altered considerably, in form and in detail, but the changes took place over a period of several years. It may have seemed to Wordsworth in 1803, as it did to Coleridge, that the line-by-line, stanza-by-stanza work on short lyric poems was keeping him from that more ample, freer mode of composition in blank verse. It is clear, at any rate, that under Coleridge's unrelenting criticism and prey to his own misgivings, Wordsworth became distressed over the relation between these short pieces and the great poem he was to write, but of which he had so far written only assorted parts.

Dorothy Wordsworth, in a letter of 1805, explains to Lady Beaumont about William's publishing "small poems." At this point, though he considered sending off "a few of the longest of them," he has given it up, she thinks, out of his "great dislike to all the business of publishing." But *his* reason, along with "many lesser objections," is his concern that "having been so long silent to the world he ought to come forward again with a work of greater labor." [11] This is said even, or perhaps especially, after the productive years

10 See John A. Finch, " 'The Ruined Cottage' Restored: Three Stages of Composition, 1795–1798," *JEGP* 66 (1967): 179–199, reprinted in *Bicentenary Wordsworth Studies*, pp. 29–49. In his doctoral dissertation, "Wordsworth, Coleridge and the Recluse: 1798–1814" (Cornell, 1964), Finch also pointed to the *Prelude's* existence first as a "two-part poem to Coleridge," later to be expanded both in content and purpose. See also Jonathan Wordsworth's study of the "two-part poem," "The Growth of a Poet's Mind," *Cornell Library Journal* 5 (1970), 3–24. For an account of "The Ruined Cottage" which takes cognizance of Finch's work, see Jonathan Wordsworth, *The Music of Humanity* (London, 1969).

11 *EY*, 1:636 (4 November 1805).

of 1804 and 1805, when Wordsworth brought the "poem on his own life" down to the years of young manhood by writing an additional eleven books. Even after he has made the decision to publish the volume of selections, he explains to Sir Walter Scott that the *Poems* (1807) "will consist entirely of small pieces" and that he will "publish with great reluctance." Wordsworth seemed always to publish reluctantly but seemed even less eager to do so at this time. For, he goes on, "the day when my long work will be finished seems farther and farther off and therefore I have resolved to send this Vol: into the world." Then, revealing his ambiguous feelings, he says, "It would look like affectation if I were to say how indifferent I am to its present reception; but I have a true pleasure in saying to you that I put some value upon it; and hope that it will one day or other be thought well of by the Public." [12] The phrase "some value" is especially telling of Wordsworth's complex attitude toward the lesser mode—a self-conscious mixture of pleasure and disdain. While offering his usual "indifference" to publication, he nevertheless expresses both how much the small poems mean to him and how "little" they are when compared to the unfinished long work.

Wordsworth could not let the matter rest. His ambivalent attitude found further and more elaborate expression in an "advertisement" he wrote as he was preparing the *Poems* (1807) for the press:

The Short Poems of which these volumes consist, were chiefly composed to refresh my mind during the progress of a work of length and labor, in which I have for some time been engaged; and to furnish me with employment when I had not resolution

12 *MY*, 2:95 (10 November 1806). We first hear of Wordsworth's decision to publish the "Volume" in a letter to Walter Scott about June 9, 1806 (Moorman, 2:96). The letter is in the Hugh Walpole Collection, National Library of Scotland.

to apply myself to that work, or hope that I should proceed with it successfully. Having already, in the Volumes entitled Lyrical Ballads, offered to the world a considerable collection of short poems, I did not wish to add these to the number, till after the completion and publication of my large work; but, as I cannot even guess when this will be, and as several of these Poems have been circulated in manuscript, I thought it better to send them forth at once. They were composed with much pleasure to my own mind, & I build upon that remembrance a hope that they may afford profitable pleasure to many readers.[13]

The poet makes more than one kind of "apology" here. The first might be paraphrased thus: I cannot publish the long poem because it is unfinished (actually, but for *The Prelude,* unwritten) in lieu of which I offer you another collection of short poems. The second reason for publishing now is born of the poet's great fear of being plagiarized: I publish these poems now to save them from being pirated, or worse, imitated before they are generally known to be mine (not an imaginary fear, but one fed by Sir Walter Scott's free use of Coleridge's "Christabel" before that poem was published). The final, most appealing explanation is an interesting reversal of the one given by Coleridge and, as I have suggested, perhaps offered by Wordsworth himself in 1803 as a rationalization for the still-sleeping long poem. Rather than a hindrance, a knot of entangling ropes, a cluster of blind alleys, a disease, the short poems become a remedy, a release, a refreshing and pleasure-giving employment arising almost in recompense for the poet's discouragement and irresolution over the "work of length and labor."

[13] Longman MS. of *Poems in Two Volumes* (1807); British Museum (MS) and Cornell Wordsworth Collection (photocopy). It was never printed by Wordsworth, but has been reproduced by W. H. White in *A Description of the Wordsworth and Coleridge Manuscripts in the Possession of Mr. T. Norton Longman* (London, 1897), pp. 71–72.

In light of the confusion of motive and veiled self-pity in the aborted "advertisement" it seems wise that Wordsworth did not publish it, whatever his reasons for not doing so. But the mere desire to include an "advertisement" of this sort reveals a need for apology, an effort to find a mask for his embarrassment. Aside from his desire to protect the poems, it, too, suggests his sense of their lesser stature compared to the unwritten *Recluse* (note for example his defensive stress upon the "profitable pleasure" the poems may afford the reader). But it reveals as well a deeper link between *The Recluse* and the small poems. Committed to a poem of severe and imposing, if vague, architectural proportions, disturbed by Coleridge's impatience at his failure to progress with it and by Coleridge's persistent criticism of the effort spent on lyric poems, Wordsworth found satisfying emotional release, spiritual bravado perhaps, in writing the short lyric poems. Not surprisingly the typical short poem deals with the very same concerns that had generated the larger work.

Later Wordsworth obscured the true relationship of small poems to large work by regarding the former as appendages to the latter, and then, when the walls would not rise of their own accord, by building what edifice he could from the smaller units. In the Preface to *The Excursion,* 1814, he spoke of the "minor Pieces" as standing in relation to *The Recluse* as do "the little Cells, Oratories and sepulchral Recesses" to a gothic cathedral. As early as 1809 he began classifying his poems according to their "primary interest." And in the *Poems* of 1815 he tried to organize them as an imitation and extension of *The Prelude,* to prepare the way as it were for that as yet unpublished "Anti-chapel" (*sic*) and its largely unwritten "gothic Church"; the purpose of the order is "to assist the attentive Reader," as he puts it in the 1815 Preface, "in perceiving their connection with each other,

HUNT LIBRARY
CARNEGIE-MELLON UNIVERSITY

and also their subordination to that Work"—that is, *The Recluse.*[14]

During the years 1799 to 1807 Wordsworth turned, off and on, to *The Recluse,* working intensively for brief periods. At Goslar in the winter of 1799 he had composed the greater part of a "two-part poem to Coleridge." These "invigorating thoughts from former years" (*Prel,* 1:649) composed primarily of the "spots of time" occasioned an elegiac response, in the Lucy and Matthew poems. Again in January 1804, he resumed work on *The Prelude.* As though in response to these labors he wrote a small but perfect set of lyrics ("I wandered lonely as a cloud," "Stepping Westward," "Solitary Reaper") and finished work on the "Immortality Ode." However, during the interim Wordsworth's efforts to sustain work on the long poem broke down. In December 1801, after a period of silence, he set out to add a third book to the "poem to Coleridge," lines preliminary to *The Recluse* itself, but the enterprise quickly played out. He then turned again to revising "The Ruined Cottage" for separate publication but soon yielded to other more pressing matters. Almost in defiance of Coleridge Wordsworth abandoned any pretense of leading others to find meaning and hope in life through his intended philosophic stance in *The Recluse.* He launched instead into a series of intensely personal lyric songs. Under the unique pressures upon him in 1802 he effectively turned his back on public "philosophic" utterance or public "healing," to use Matthew Arnold's word, and did what he could in the way of personal therapy.

With time Wordsworth developed a theory of poetic expression which followed his own practice. The famous passage from the 1800 Preface on "emotion recollected in tran-

[14] *LCW,* 128, 140; *EY,* 1:594 (3 June 1805); *MY,* 2:334-336 (5 May 1809).

quillity" is difficult to analyze but clear in general intent: the poet moves through his several "consciousnesses" in order to get at the one that demands expression. This process can be a labored series of meditational steps, as he describes it in 1800. Or it can be a sudden discovery. Wordsworth's pronouncement to De Quincey in 1809 suggests the second form.

De Quincey tells of an occasion when he and Wordsworth were waiting impatiently for news of "the Peninsular war," brought by carrier late at night. Wordsworth put his ear to the road to listen for the sound of the approaching wheels, doing so with great concentration. As he rose, having heard nothing, he noticed a bright star on the horizon. He then told De Quincey:

I have remarked, from my earliest days, that, if under any circumstances the attention is energetically braced up to an act of steady observation, or of steady expectation, then, if this intense condition of vigilance should suddenly relax at that moment any beautiful, any impressive visual object, or collection of objects, falling upon the eye, is carried to the heart with a power not known under other circumstances. Just now, my ear was placed upon the stretch, in order to catch any sound of wheels that might come down upon the lake of Wythburn from the Keswick road; at the very instant when I raised my head from the ground, in final abandonment of hope for this night, at the very instant when the organs of attention were all at once relaxing from their tension, the bright star hanging in the air above those outlines of massy blackness fell suddenly upon my eye, and penetrated my capacity of apprehension with a pathos and a sense of the infinite, that would not have arrested me under other circumstances.[15]

[15] *Recollections of the Lake Poets,* ed. E. Sackville-West (London, 1948), pp. 143–144, as first printed in *Tait's Edinburgh Magazine* 6 (1839): 94. De Quincey later revised the Wordsworth pieces exten-

De Quincey tells the story in defense of Wordsworth's poem "There Was a Boy" (*PW*, 2:206), a connection, he tells us, Wordsworth himself had made at the time of the incident. The boy, too, lost in concentrated listening, undergoes an epiphanic vision.

"There Was a Boy" and the kind of experience it emblemizes was to take a prominent place in the elaborate arrangement of his poems that the poet began making in the same year as his conversation with De Quincey. Wordsworth explains, in the Preface to *Poems* (1815), where he discusses the new arrangement of his poems into categories, that he has begun "the series of Poems placed under the head of Imagination . . . with one of the earliest processes of Nature in the development of this faculty."

Guided by one of my own primary consciousnesses, I have represented a commutation and transfer of internal feelings, cooperating with external accidents to plant, for immortality, images of sound and sight, in the celestial soil of the Imagination. The Boy, there introduced, is listening, with something of a feverish and restless anxiety, for the recurrence of the riotous sounds which he had previously excited; and, at the moment when the intenseness of his mind is beginning to remit, he is surprised into a perception of the solemn and tranquillizing images which the Poem describes.[16]

Wordsworth has written of other incidents, in *The Prelude* especially, which parallel this of the boy (who is Wordsworth

---

sively and omitted this and many other passages when preparing the collected edition of his works. He gives no date, but 1809 is the time of Wordsworth's tract, *Concerning . . . the Convention of Cintra*, which had to do with "the Peninsular war" and the subsequent treatment of the French by the English commanders. De Quincey helped ready the manuscript for the press. See Moorman, 2:138ff.

[16] *LCW*, 151, 152. Wordsworth also used the lines in *Prel*, 5:389–413.

himself in an early version of the poem).[17] The snaring of woodcocks, the Simplon Pass episode (in a delayed reaction), and the ascent of Mount Snowdon are some of the incidents which share the characteristic swing from intense concentration to a vision, a release from former vigilance, usually lyric in the manner of its expression.[18]

Other poets have known similar experiences. The quest for images that will ease "the burden of the mystery" is confined neither to Wordsworth alone nor to the Romantics as a group. Coleridge might be said to have invented the mode: the mind casually plays with its immediate surroundings until it apprehends through heightened language an important phase in the history of its consciousness. But especially in the poetry of Wordsworth, and also of Keats, the movement of mind proceeds from preoccupation, whether in playfulness, "dreamy indifference," "anxiety," or "vigilance," through sudden wakefulness—often a passive but receptive state—and on to vision with its renewed and transcendent intensity. Consider Keats as a parallel instance. Keats in the introduction to "The Fall of Hyperion" is disturbed by the relation between dreamer and poet, without ever fully defining it or resolving the dilemma it causes. But from initial listlessness, a mood which belies deep anxiety and uncertainty, the dreamer ascends through alert passiveness to vision.[19] Moreover, like Wordsworth, Keats failed to progress

[17] *Prel*, pp. 639–640, Appendix, MS. JJ.

[18] See Jonathan Bishop, "Wordsworth and the 'Spots of Time,' " *ELH* 26 (1959): 45–65. Several of the "spots of time" have this general design implicit in the experiences they describe: the skating and stolen boat episodes, the Discharged Soldier (considered as the climax to a narrative unit beginning with the riotous dance). Bishop describes the design as a combination of a repeated action (concentration) and the emergence of a solitary figure from a crowd (vision), pp. 46, 47.

[19] Keats transmutes the experience into dream-allegory or mythic vision. See the "forgetfulness" of Canto I, lines 102–105, the terrible

with the "large work." "Hyperion: A Fragment" and the second effort, "The Fall of Hyperion," are poems planned on an epic scale. When the project halted in April 1819, Keats turned away to the lyric odes of the *annus mirabilis*. Again like Wordsworth, he regarded his lyrics as lesser poems and the unfinished "Hyperion" as a major poetic effort. Of long poems, Keats wrote to Benjamin Bailey, "The Lovers of Poetry like to have a little Region to wander in." He then added in Keatsian hyperbole, "Did our great Poets ever write short Pieces?" [20] But like Wordsworth, Keats did write short pieces when stymied by long ones. This very pattern was characteristic of Wordsworth's mode of composition during the spring of 1802, when unable to sustain both impulses he let the lyric one have free rein. In both cases, the lyric voice takes up the same "burden" but in different form.

The spring of 1802 is for Wordsworth a period of great uncertainty and momentous decision, of intense delight and anxious doubt and disappointment. It was a time when not only the poem on his own life lay fallow and seemed threatened by silence, but his way of life and its emotional and spiritual continuity suddenly faltered, under the new internal and external pressures, under his deep sense of changes within himself, and under his awareness of shifting relationships with persons both near and distant. The strange and

---

concentration (118–120), its consequent "chill" (122), and the poet's struggle "to escape the numbness" (127–128). At the touch of the lowest stair life surges back (132–134) and the poet encounters the veiled Moneta (136ff.), who finally "parted the veils" (256) (*The Poetical Works of John Keats*, ed. H. W. Garrod, 2d ed. [London, 1958], 511–516).

20 *The Letters of John Keats 1814–1821*, ed. Hyder Rollins (Cambridge, Mass., 1958), 1:170 (8 October 1817).

desperate isolation at Goslar in the winter of 1799 turned Wordsworth's mind back to memories of childhood. In that strained time, hard to fathom because so little is known about it, Wordsworth began to work steadily on the "poem to Coleridge" and found vent for the lyric impulse in the Lucy and Matthew elegies. Three years later, now home at Grasmere, Wordsworth is again confronted with himself, with the links between past and present, and their effect on his future. Having written little of *The Recluse* in the interval and unable to make any further progress with the poem "on his early life,"[21] he writes nearly thirty lyric poems. None are elegies, but nearly all have to do, whatever their mood, with the uses made of the personal past in deriving meaning in the present, and hope for the future. That spring is one of the poetically richest times in Wordsworth's career.

A brief description of the poems is in order before we proceed. As for long poems, he tried unsuccessfully to rework "The Ruined Cottage," which he now called "The Pedlar," and to add to the "poem to Coleridge." But early

---

[21] "Home at Grasmere," as John A. Finch has argued, was begun in 1800 but may have been written largely in 1806–1807 ("On the Dating of *Home at Grasmere:* A New Approach," *Bicentenary Wordsworth Studies,* pp. 14–28). The years between Wordsworth's return to Grasmere in 1800 and the spring of 1802 are thus revealed as quite barren of extended composition. One reason, perhaps, for the poet's burst of activity from 1804 to 1807, after his poem's long sleep, was that he needed to work through certain problems piecemeal, as it were, in the lyrics, and then in the sonnets written during the next year, before he could deal with them on a large scale in the long poem (that is in *The Prelude* and "Home at Grasmere," both thought of as parts of *The Recluse*). See also Finch's article, "Wordsworth's Two-Handed Engine," on the dating of the "glad preamble," in *Bicentenary Wordsworth Studies,* pp. 1–13.

in March he wrote four lyrical ballads which focus upon the poet's encounter, expressed or implied, with a "character": "The Sailor's Mother" (first called "The Singing Bird"), "Alice Fell, or Poverty," "Beggars," and "The Emigrant Mother." It is just possible, too, that "The Affliction of Margaret," whose heroine was first called Mary, and "The Forsaken," the latter an "overflow" from the former poem, were written early in the year as additions to *Lyrical Ballads,* even though these "dramatic monologues" are less colloquial, more "literary," more syntactically sophisticated, than "Alice Fell," "Beggars," or "The Sailor's Mother." "Repentance: A Pastoral" appears among manuscripts associated with this period and may also have been written along with the rest. If so, all the poems may have originally been intended for the new two-volume edition of *Lyrical Ballads* but were held back, perhaps, in deference to the extensive additions to the Preface.

The earliest version of "The Leech-Gatherer," from the point of view of technique, belongs in this group, too, though it was begun too late for inclusion in *Lyrical Ballads.* In the later version the ballad features are toned down or eliminated altogether, but the first version seems to have been conceived in this genre. (See Chapter 6.) Another "character" poem, "The Tinker," written late in April, does not share the pathos and mood of "affliction" found in the first group, but is instead an attempt at light-hearted characterization in quite another vein.[22]

22 *PW,* 4:366. Some of the lightness and verve of the ballad called "The Tinker" in Joseph Ritson's *Ancient Songs from Henry III to the Revolution* (1790) is reproduced in Wordsworth's "Tinker." The book appears in the catalogue of his library at Rydal Mount which was made up by Dora Wordsworth in 1829. This MS catalogue is now in Harvard College Library.

After writing the first group of ballads, Wordsworth, in mid-March, began a series of lyrics distinctive in tone and manner, unlike anything he had done before. They are different in kind from the blank-verse lyrics written in 1797–1798, "Lines left upon a seat" and "Tintern Abbey," for example, the form for which he is best known. Geoffrey Hartman has traced the roots of this earlier "free standing poem" to the eighteenth-century inscription and the ancient (that is, the more elegiac and expansive) epigram, which is "liberated" by the poet in such a way that the "form appears to be self-generated rather than prompted by tradition." Hartman also shows that the lyric productions of 1799 at Goslar, the Lucy poems in particular, may be seen as a development and purification of this epigrammatic form.[23]

It is commonplace to associate Burns's nature lyrics, like "To a Mountain Daisy," with Wordsworth's lyrics of 1802, usually typified by his "To a Daisy." Wordsworth admired Burns; and in many tributes to him, in verse and in prose, he freely acknowledged his debt and praised Burns's "simplicity," "Truth," and "vigour." Nevertheless it is a rare occasion when Wordsworth openly imitates the older poet or shows more than the most superficial sign of "influence": a borrowed phrase, a quoted line or two, an experiment in a bumptious narrative style reminiscent of "Tam O Shanter."[24]

[23] "Wordsworth, Inscriptions, and Romantic Nature Poetry," in *From Sensibility to Romanticism: Essays Presented to Frederick A. Pottle*, ed. F. H. Hilles and H. Bloom (Oxford, 1965), pp. 391, 402–404. See also his *Wordsworth's Poetry, 1787–1814* (New Haven, 1964), pp. 151–162.

[24] *PW*, 3:442. See Russell Noyes, "Wordsworth and Burns," *PMLA* 59 (1944): 813–832. Noyes defines the period of Burns's "influence" on Wordsworth as 1798 to 1805, that influence coming "virtually to an end" with "The Waggoner" (p. 824). But even during this period when Wordsworth was writing a great many lyrics of all kinds, Burns's

An explanation for Wordsworth's "debt" that seems far more likely than direct influence is the younger poet's shock of recognition at discovering Burns, his delight in hearing a natural voice singing poems of place, it is true, neither his song nor his place, but kindred nevertheless. Then, too, both poets look back, ultimately, to similar traditions. If the lyrics of 1802 have a generic ancestor it must be sought among the lyric poems of the sixteenth and seventeenth centuries rather than those of the eighteenth.[25]

Wordsworth came nearest to the special quality of the 1802 poems in the set of poems written in 1798 ("Expostulation and Reply," "The Tables Turned," and "To My Sister"), noticed by Mary Moorman for their "joyousness." [26] They are unique among his poems up to that time; their ballad-like form (aba^4b^3) and their exaggerated, almost raucous tone, in strange combination with a strong doctrinal element, keep them distinct, despite their concern with "human renovation." [27] But, with one exception to be discussed later,

lyrics are noticeably "echoed" in only the slightest ways. See also Raymond Bentman, "The Romantic Poets and Critics on Robert Burns," *Texas Studies in Literature and Language* 6 (1964): 104–118, for a convenient gathering of romantic views on Burns.

[25] See my article "Wordsworth and English Poetry of the Sixteenth and Seventeenth Centuries," *Cornell Library Journal* 1 (1966): 28–39.

[26] Moorman, 1:381. William Heath points out an antecedent in "The whirl-blast from behind the hill" (*PW*, 2:127, 128) in its earliest form (1798; *Wordsworth and Coleridge: A Study of Their Literary Relations, 1801–1802* [Oxford, 1970], p. 57).

[27] The poems are "To My Sister," "Lines Written in Early Spring," "Expostulation and Reply," "Tables Turned," and "Lines written at a small distance from my house." Hartman writes in *Wordsworth's Poetry* that the "true subject of the credal lyrics," that is the poems listed here, "is rebirth—human renovation—and that depends on whether the heart can still give itself as in youth" (p. 153). Compared, for example, to the "Lucy" poems, these poems surprise by overstatement rather than by understatement.

22

nothing the poet wrote before February 1802 quite prepares us for the lyrics of that spring.

BIBLIOGRAPHICAL NOTE

Most critics have acknowledged the crisis in 1802, but few agree on it causes, an indication perhaps of its depth and complexity. George M. Harper found the years 1800 to 1802 the time "when the political contradictions in [Wordsworth's] heart," those between his patriotism and his revolutionary hopes, "had ceased to torture him" and he was free to enter upon a "new era of poetic productiveness" (*Willam Wordsworth: His Life, Works and Influence* [London, 1916; reprinted New York, 1960], 2:355). Helen Darbishire refined Harper's distinction between the material of *Lyrical Ballads* (1798) and that of *Poems in Two Volumes* (1807). The "effort of projection" in the first book, she writes, which carried him "by a strenuous act of imagination into the 'deep heart of man' and the inner life of Nature," could not be sustained. Wordsworth, in 1802, "returned into himself . . . and approached his poetic experience from that centre" (*William Wordsworth, Poems in Two Volumes, 1807* [Oxford, 1914; rev. ed., 1952], Introduction, p. xl). More recently F. W. Bateson has suggested that Wordsworth wrote the lyrics of 1802, many connected with his sister Dorothy in some way, to persuade her that "she was the one he really loved," to make his marriage with Mary Hutchinson seem "less intolerable" (*Wordsworth: A Re-Interpretation* [London, 1956], p. 159). Though right in his perception that Wordsworth's crisis was a real one, Bateson fails to recognize that it was a complex one. Since Bateson's study attention has been focused more intently on the poems and their immediate contexts. Alan Grob has found, during this crucial period, a conflict of "two major orthodoxies" in Wordsworth's mind: that between his faith as "essentially naturalistic" and his vision as "fundamentally transcendental." Poems the subject of which is the "loss of vital imaginative faculty" stand against those concerned with "the enlargement of natural and moral

23

awareness" (Wordsworth's 'Immortality Ode' and the Search for Identity," *ELH* 32 [1965]: 32). Working from a different premise toward similar conclusions, Geoffrey H. Hartman finds evidence in the "Immortality Ode," *The Prelude,* and "Resolution and Independence" that Wordsworth questions "whether the 'marvelous Boy' in him can survive being changed into the 'philosophic mind,' whether poetry must die with maturation." Although a "lesser danger" lies in the suppression of creative powers by day-to-day concerns, "the real concern is that they might be displaced from life and become apocalyptic" (*Wordsworth's Poetry, 1787–1814* [New Haven, 1964], p. 203).

Nearly eveyone else who discusses the "Immortality Ode" or "Resolution and Independence," whether he adduces biographical evidence or not, finds in the one or the other poem the signs of a crisis, either of "growing old" or of "growing up," as Lionel Trilling has so aptly put it (*The Liberal Imagination* [Garden City, N.Y., 1950], p. 127).

Odd as it may seem, however, many have treated the period as an unusually blissful one. Ernest de Selincourt in his essay on Coleridge's "Dejection: An Ode" (*Wordsworthian and Other Essays* [Oxford, 1947]) emphasizes Wordsworth's happiness as it plays against Coleridge's disappointments and despair, though he tempers this view somewhat in his *Dorothy Wordsworth: A Biography* (Oxford, 1933), pp. 140–143. H. M. Margoliouth in *Wordsworth and Coleridge 1795–1835* (London, 1953) speaks (p. 104) of Wordsworth's "quite unnecessary seriousness" during this period (referring to "Resolution and Independence"). Mary Moorman, though she mentions most of the details, seems to miss the outline of Wordsworth's experience (Moorman, 1:501–588). Wallace W. Douglas, in *Wordsworth: The Construction of a Personality* (Kent, Ohio, 1968), has analyzed the early years of Wordsworth's life as preparation for the "completed" personality he was to achieve at Grasmere, essentially in December 1799, when he moved there with his sister Dorothy, and more fully in 1802 when the "beautiful society" Coleridge so often talked about was finally established (p. 175). Douglas' emphasis, of course, is on the early years, but his assumptions about the period after 1799 are puzzling, given the evidence.

The emphasis Douglas puts on Coleridge is significant. Earl Leslie Griggs, in an attempt to see "Wordsworth through Coleridge's eyes," comes to regard 1802 as climactic in the relations between the two poets. During the years after the second edition of the *Lyrical Ballads* (1800), Griggs finds that Coleridge's "achievement . . . is pathetic" for several reasons: his "volitional paralysis"; his residence in the north, with direct effect upon his ill health, and through the latter upon his increasing consumption of opium; the discord and frustration over his relations with Sara Hutchinson; and Wordsworth's "failure to appreciate his poetry and give him the encouragement he needed"; all this, and especially the last, "undermined his self-confidence" and led to "Dejection: An Ode," which, in its first form as a letter to Sara Hutchinson, might well be regarded as a pathetic document ("Wordsworth through Coleridge's Eyes," in *Wordsworth: Centenary Studies* [Princeton, 1951], pp. 61–63). See also A. M. Buchan, "The Influence of Wordsworth on Coleridge (1795–1800)," *University of Toronto Quarterly* 32 (1963): 346–366. But Coleridge through Wordsworth's eyes could not have been a heartening sight (C. M. Bowra attributes a great part of the cause for the crisis to Wordsworth's concern for Coleridge, in *The Romantic Imagination* [Cambridge, Mass., 1949], pp. 85–93). Both the "Immortality Ode" and "Resolution and Independence" are part of a poetic dialogue on despair that took place between the two poets early in 1802. There is good reason to regard Coleridge's "Letter to [Asra]," the first version of "Dejection: An Ode," as a response to Wordsworth's "Immortality Ode" (what had been written by April 3); and "Resolution and Independence," in some way an answer to the "Letter to [Asra]," is in turn answered by Coleridge's revised "Dejection." The most recent and the most detailed treatment of the relations between the two poets during this period is by William Heath in *Wordsworth and Coleridge: A Study of Their Literary Relations, 1801–1802* (Oxford, 1970). In his attempt to "be the builder of another context within which great art can be read," the author covers much of the same ground covered in this and the following chapters. As his subtitle indicates, however, his emphasis is upon the "literary relations" between the two men, primarily from the viewpoint of a biographer. Though he discusses Wordsworth's search for and discovery of "authenticity— a style," he does so in different terms and comes to quite different conclusions from those of this book. He sees the poems less as poems in their own right than as expressions of a complex and richly human experience. Heath suggests convincingly that the revised "Dejection, Etc." addressed to William ("Edmund") and published on Wordsworth's wedding day (4 October 1802) is Coleridge's reply to "Resolution and Independence" (p. 164). David Pirie has made an exhaustive chronological study of Coleridge's revisions of the poem in *"A Letter to [Asra]," Bicentenary Wordsworth Studies in Memory of John Alban Finch,* edited by Jonathan Wordsworth and Beth Darlington (Ithaca and London, 1970), pp. 294–339. See also studies by Newton P. Stallknecht, "The Doctrine of Coleridge's 'Dejection' and Its Relation to Wordsworth's Philosophy," *PMLA* 49 (1934): 196–207; George W. Meyer, " 'Resolution and Independence': Wordsworth's Answer to Coleridge's 'Dejection: An Ode,' " *Tulane Studies in English* 2 (1950): 49–74; Humphrey House, *Coleridge* (London, 1953), pp. 133–141; George Whalley, *Coleridge and Sara Hutchinson and the Asra Poems* (Toronto, 1953); George Watson, *Coleridge the Poet* (London, 1966), pp. 77–80; and Geoffrey Yarlott, *Coleridge and the Abyssinian Maid* (London, 1967), pp. 244–279.

[2]

Old Accents and
the New Voice

The first poems Wordsworth wrote in March of 1802 were ballads, further accents of a voice already established in 1798. Before turning to the new lyrics we will consider the poems of this familiar mode. Three poems, "The Sailor's Mother," "Alice Fell," and "Beggars," depict a meeting between the poet-traveller and a counter-figure, a wandering and usually alien spirit, whose "story," either elicited from her or willingly told, stands in sharp contrast to the poet's experience, giving him pause. The emphasis in these poems falls on the startling self-sufficiency of the wanderers and their gift for effective speech. They are reminiscent of such poems from the *Lyrical Ballads* of 1798 as "The Last of the Flock" and "We Are Seven," though they lack the doctrinaire edge common to the *Ballads*.

"The Emigrant Mother," composed in mid-March, and three other poems that may have been written about the same time, "The Affliction of Mary —— of ——," its off-shoot, "The Forsaken," and "Repentance," are all dramatic monologues in the manner of "The Mad Mother," "The Complaint of a Forsaken Indian Woman," and "The Last of the Flock." Like the last three mentioned from *Lyrical*

Ballads, the new ballads have to do with the psychological effects of loss. Unlike the earlier poems, they lack any introductory narrative frame or verifying explanation. As first written they depend wholly on the revelatory powers of the speaker's voice for their effect. "The Emigrant Mother" suffers from excessive length, perhaps the result of the speaker's self-punishing desire to prompt and draw out her grief.

> My own dear Harry he will sigh
> Sweet Babe! and they will let him die.
> "He pines" they'll say "it is his doom,
> And you may see his day is come."
> O! had he but thy chearful smiles
> Limbs stout as thine, and lips as gay,
> These looks, thy cunning and thy wiles
> And countenance like a summer's day,
> They would have hopes of him, and then
> I should behold his face again.   [31–40]

In revising the poem Wordsworth does not seek to compress the effects of the mother's loss into fewer lines, but instead "allows" her self-indulgence by establishing a narrative framework based on his supposed difficulties in translating from the French and on the subterfuge of eavesdropping.

"Repentance, A Pastoral Ballad," as it was called when published for the first time in 1820, shows greater skill. The long rushing lines of anapestic tetrameter, with effective variation of the initial foot, give expression to the speaker's compulsive garrulousness, but the tightly-rhymed quatrains, unlike the longer ten-line stanzas of "The Emigrant Mother," control the speaker's utterance.

> O Fools that we were we had land which we sold;
> Half a dozen snug fields, fat, contented, and gay;
> They'd have done us more good than another man's gold,
> Could we but have been as contented as they.   [1–4]

The woman's simpleness slips into bathos at times:

> O Thomas! O Thomas! come sunshine come shower
> Where's your bustle, your business, your joy & your pride.
>
> [9–12]

But the same simple manner of speaking is used with great skill in the following lines:

> When my sick crazy body had lain without sleep,
> What a comfort at sunrise it was when I stood
> And look'd down on the fields and the Cows & the Sheep
> From the top of the hill, 'twas like youth in my blood.
>
> [25–28]

"The Affliction of Mary —— of ——" is perhaps the most powerful and moving poem of the ones so far discussed:

> My apprehensions come in crowds;
> I dread the rustling of the grass;
> The very shadows of the clouds
> Have power to shake me as they pass:
> I question things, and do not find
> One that will answer to my mind;
> And all the world appears unkind. [64–70]

Wordsworth's success here springs from his ability to enter into the imagination and feelings of such a woman, speaking not as she literally spoke, but as her inner being must have striven to speak. This differentiates her both from the other monologuists and from the wanderers and vagrants who speak their pain without ever fully expressing it. The imaginative perception of their suffering is left to the reader, who is led to encounter the dramatic surprise of the narrative by the poet, not by the speaker. "Resolution and Independence," to be discussed fully in Chapter 6, brings certain elements of these 1802 "ballads" into perfect balance with new accents just emerging. To an examination of these accents we now turn.

On the 14th of March, 1802, Wordsworth wrote the first poem to the Butterfly, "Stay near me," and thus began the unique series of lyrics which marked out a new direction. In 1807, he did not regard the entire set of poems as a coherent whole deserving a special section in *Poems in Two Volumes*. Eight are omitted entirely; six appear in the first mixed group of poems, containing lyrical ballads, meditative poems, narratives, and an ode; and four more are included in a shorter mixed group that concludes the second volume. But eight are grouped homogeneously with five later lyrics in a section called, as though in warning, "Moods of My Own Mind." [1] This last group, made up of poems more nearly alike in form and in theme than any other section, and quite unlike the ballads in the familiar pattern discussed above, drew the attention and ire of reviewers and contemporary readers. So strong was the outcry, and so earnest was Wordsworth's response, that an examination of

---

[1] Three of the eight poems (excluding "The Tinker")—"These chairs they have no words to utter," "I have been here in the Moonlight," and "The Barberry Tree"—were never published by the poet. "A Farewell" and "Stanzas" were published in 1815, "The Forsaken" not until 1842. "Travelling" never appeared as a separate poem, but lines from it were used in a sequel to "Ode to Lycoris," published in 1820 (*PW*, 4:97–98). The contents of "Moods of My Own Mind" are: the first "To a Butterfly," "The Sun has long been set," "Written in March," "O Nightingale! thou surely art," "My heart leaps up," "Pleasures newly found," "I wandered lonely as a Cloud," "Who fancied what a pretty sight," "The Sparrow's Nest," "Gipsies," "To the Cuckoo," the second "To a Butterfly," and "It is no Spirit who from Heaven hath flown."

this debate will help to define Wordsworth's sense of the unique voice he was adopting.

Sir Walter Scott sensed the singularity of these lyrics when he called them *"caviare,* not only to the multitude, but to all who judge of poetry by the established rules of criticism." [2] But the principal complaint is against Wordsworth's " 'abandoning' his mind to the most commonplace ideas," as Byron put it, adding acidly, "clothing them in language not simple but puerile." [3] Anna Seward's unsympathetic and amusing paraphrase of "I wandered lonely as a cloud," strikes even deeper. She is especially irked at the poet's detailing what he himself called the "fluxes and refluxes" of his mind, "in the hours," as she puts it, "of pensive or of pained contemplation." But the singular quality of "I wandered" exercises her indignation, for she greatly admires "Resolution and Independence" and the "Immortality Ode" (though only the first five stanzas).[4] Both these poems are based on the inner journeyings of the poet's mind. What she was evidently prepared to accept in "Resolution and Independence" was its drawing a generalized moral sentiment from a natural scene. The wandering mind turning back upon itself is finally supplanted by the almost trite reflection, "God . . . be my

[2] Scott to Southey, *The Letters of Sir Walter Scott,* ed. H. C. Grierson (London, 1932), 1:390. Robert Jeffrey, whom Scott mentions in his letter to Southey, poured vitriol over both volumes in his review of *Poems in Two Volumes (Edinburgh Review,* 11 [1807]: 214ff).

[3] Review of *Poems in Two Volumes, Monthly Literary Recreations,* July 1807 (quoted by Elsie Smith, *An Estimate of William Wordsworth by his Contemporaries, 1793–1822* [Oxford, 1932], pp. 70–72). With Byronic scorn he compares "Written in March" ("The cock is crowing," etc.) with "Hey de diddle. The cat and the fiddle."

[4] *Letters of Anna Seward, Written between the Years 1784 and 1807,* 6 vols. (Edinburgh, 1811), 6:366–367. Quoted in part by Hartman, *Wordsworth's Poetry,* p. 4.

help and stay secure! / I'll think of the Leech-gatherer on the lonely Moor." The Daffodil poem, however, cannot be so neatly rescued by Mrs. Seward.[5]

What irritated readers and reviewers was not the illusion of intimacy in lyric verse, nor the poet having "suck'd divinity from flowers." [6] They recognized these traditional modes in English verse, but were astonished by Wordsworth's deliberate emphasis upon the movements of his *own* mind and the great significance he assigned to them. They felt danger in private moods laid open to the public, for in such moods the poet sees too much in too little, manufactures, according to Anna Seward, "metaphysic importance upon trivial themes," finds spiritual rebirth in a cuckoo's song or in a host of daffodils. Moreover, the "lesser poems" are the more "caviare" because they stand next to and seem

[5] There were defenders. William Hazlitt was not always the bear toward "trifles" that he pretended to be. In *The Spirit of the Age* (1825) he writes, "No one has shown the same imagination in raising trifles into importance: no one has displayed the same pathos in treating of the simplest feelings of the heart" as Wordsworth has done (*Complete Works*, ed. P. P. Howe [London and Toronto, 1930–1934], 11:88, 89). In this book and elsewhere he has high praise for "To the Cuckoo" and "To the Daisy" and for "part of the Leech-gatherer": "They open a finer and deeper vein of thought and feeling than any poet in modern times has done, or attempted" (5:156). Walter Bagehot has observed that in the lyric poem Wordsworth and other "such self-describing poets, describe what is *in* them, but not peculiar to them,—what is generic, not what is special and individual" (in "Wordsworth, Tennyson, and Browning, or Pure, Ornate, and Grotesque Art in Poetry," *National Review*, N.S. 1 [November 1864]: 34.)

[6] The magazines were full of poetry which pretended to be of the intimate, autobiographical kind. See Robert Mayo, "The Contemporaneity of the *Lyrical Ballads*," *PMLA* 69 (1954): 490–494, 516. Part of the shock of Wordsworth's verse was its deliberate cutting away of pretense.

to vie for attention with the works of a more substantial nature, indeed, seem to claim as much or more. The frequent use of imperatives in the little poems ("Look! . . . Behold!"), or of invocations ("O blessed Bird! . . . O life . . . Child of the Year! . . . Bright Flower! . . . Sweet Flower! . . . Thou, Linnet! . . . Drunken Lark!") and the consistent use of the formal "thee" and "thou," signal the weight the poet makes these poems bear.

After the volumes were published Wordsworth received, through Lady Beaumont, the common, almost universal, complaint, this time from the poet Samuel Rogers, "that so many trifling things should be admitted to obstruct the view of those that have merit." The poet deals with this criticism of his "little poems" in his reply to Lady Beaumont (21 May 1807). Conscious, perhaps, that his words would spread to a wider audience, he is at pains to point out to Lady Beaumont how the sonnets on "Liberty" and in particular the "Moods" make up coherent and meaningful units. Of the "Moods" he writes,

There is scarcely a Poem here of above thirty Lines, and very trifling these poems will appear to many; but, omitting to speak of them individually, do they not, taken collectively, fix the attention upon a subject eminently poetical, viz., the interest which objects in nature derive from the predominance of certain affections more or less permanent, more or less capable of salutary renewal in the mind of the being contemplating these objects?

He then adds, for emphasis, "This is poetic, and essentially poetic, and why? because it is creative." [7] In this semi-public statement he counters the argument of his critics by finding permanent affections in what must seem only trifling to the

[7] *MY*, 2:147.

inattentive reader. Typically the "objects" themselves are not interesting; they accrue interest only as the contemplating mind of the poet lights upon them. He also seeks to overcome the charge of triviality by placing poems in groups —by insisting, in an extension of his earlier advice, on their collective force.

However, his sense of their intimacy is sustained in less public statements. Before his critics erupted, Wordsworth had speculated on the proper way to read his new volumes. He felt that "there is no forming a true estimate of a volume of *small* poems by reading them all together; one stands in the way of the other." He suggested further that "they must either be read a few at once, or the book must remain some time by one, before a judgment can be made of the quantity of thought and feeling and imagery it contains, and what (and what variety of) moods of mind it can either impart or is suited to." [8] Aware of the great range in form, in feeling, and in degree of seriousness in *Poems* (1807), quite in contrast to the earlier *Lyrical Ballads,* Wordsworth strongly recommended that each poem be read for itself, in its own proper "mood of mind."

A short time after publication, in a letter to his good friend the Rev. Francis Wrangham, he offsets the critical reaction to his poems by pointing to two lines of the Daffodil poem,

> They flash upon that inward eye
> Which is the bliss of Solitude. [15–16]

"which if thoroughly felt," he writes, "would annihilate nine tenths of the Reviews of the Kingdom, as they would find no Readers." [9] Wordsworth attempts in these phrases, "to refresh my mind," "mood of mind," "inward eye," and

[8] *MY,* 2:95, 10 November 1806. [9] *MY,* 2:174, 4 November 1807.

even the pompous "salutary renewal," to reinforce our sense of the individual value of each poem. The phrases point to the deep springs of the poet's lyric expression. And they suggest a way in which he intended these poems to be read, a way hidden by his "published" advice to Lady Beaumont.

I have already described Wordsworth's characteristic habits of poetic composition—a rhythmic flow from creative activity to restorative repose—and suggested a link between the experience of composing poetry and the very pattern of the verse itself. The incident, related by De Quincey, of Wordsworth's sighting the "bright star" on the Keswick road, and the analogues provided by Wordsworth himself in "There Was a Boy" and throughout *The Prelude,* in which the poet is "surprized into a perception," display the nature of the psychological process and suggest the ordonnance for its poetic expression. For in Wordsworth's poetry the mind uses itself for its own stimulus, playfully toying with the images it holds or sees in prospect. The mind is then drawn out of or "awakened" from its former ill-defined or ambiguous state, is, in fact, overcome by the power of its own recollection or vision, ending finally in rest.

Wordsworth discusses this existential process or movement of mind in two passages, one dating from 1800, the other from 1807. In the first, he comments upon "To Joanna," one of the "Poems on the Naming of Places." In this poem the mood is complicated by the presence of an unsympathetic auditor, the Vicar, to whom the poet reacts, while he also responds to the rock and to the memory of a former visit there with "Joanna." The pattern he describes is clear, nevertheless. He begins in diversion and "play," then responds to the very "images of beauty in the description" that he is drawing for the Vicar; his mind is "softened" by them and forgets its initial purpose. He is caught in the "trap" of his own imagining, "takes fire," and enters a dream-like "trance," a "fit of imagination," a vision filled with "tumult." He wakens, again acknowledges the Vicar's presence, and ends "in a deep strain of tenderness."

What is especially significant about this passage is its effort to create a sense of tone, or voice; and what is remarkable about the voice described is its playfulness, its openness to its own creations. After "waking," Wordsworth writes, the poet of "To Joanna" tells "the story as it happened really." But not quite, for he also tells it, he says, "as the recollection of it exists permanently & regularly in my mind, mingling allusions suffused with humor, partly to the trance in which I have been, & partly to the trick I have been playing on the Vicar." [10] "To Joanna," of course, is a blank verse lyric written in 1800. But more than any other lyric written before 1802, it shares certain important features with the lyrics in question. It would easily qualify as one of the "Moods of My Own Mind." Like them it has to do with the rejuvenating power of objects in nature. A distilled essence of the type, as Wordsworth pointed out to Wrangham, can be found in the Daffodil poem. What is unique, it seems to me, is that Wordsworth should choose, as he did in "To Joanna," the light and partly playful lyric voice to carry this important strain, tied up as it is both with memory and with youth. A glance at the shorter 1802 lyrics outside the "Moods of My Own Mind" reveals that they, too, fit the description given by Wordsworth in his letter to Lady Beaumont quoted above. Again, like "To Joanna," they all

[10] From DCP, MS Verse 35, between the second and third parts of *Peter Bell* (MS 2). It appears to date from 1800 when "To Joanna" was composed; but as two pages are cut away from the MS in the middle of the passage, while no break occurs in its continuity, it might have been written in at a later time. See *PW*, 2:112, 487.

treat of "trifling" incidents or objects in the present, or in the near or distant past. They show Wordsworth observing "affinities / In objects where no brotherhood exists / To passive minds" (*Prel*, 2:384–386 [1850]). They, in his sense, are "essentially poetic" because they are "creative," creative in that they "call forth and . . . communicate power," [11] though of a subdued kind and in an unweighted voice.

In the 1807 letter to Lady Beaumont, Wordsworth discusses at some length the sonnet, "With Ships the sea was sprinkled far and nigh," composed probably in the summer or fall of 1802. He first lays down a general psychological principle, or "law of thought":

Who is there that has not felt that the mind can have no rest among a multitude of objects, of which it either cannot make one whole, or from which it cannot single out one individual, whereupon may be concentrated the attention divided among or distracted by a multitude? After a certain time we must either select one image or object, which must put out of view the rest wholly, or must subordinate them to itself while it stands forth as a Head.

He then describes how in the very act of composing the sonnet his mind moves from "dreamy indifference" to the image of a "multitude of Ships," out of this "pleasurable state of feelings" into "a kind of comparative listlessness or apathy." Suddenly, "comes forth an object, an individual," and his mind, "sleepy and unfixed, is awakened and fastened in a moment." The ship comes "upon a mission of the poetic Spirit," because in itself, Wordsworth stresses, "the ship is barely sufficiently distinguished to rouse the creative faculty." The human mind, he reflects, is open "to exertions at all times" but "doubly so when they come upon us in a state

<hr />

[11] "Essay, Supplementary to the Preface" (1815), *LCW*, 184.

of remissness." In what follows in the sonnet his "mind wantons with grateful joy in the exercise of its own powers." It loves its own creation, "making her a sovereign . . . and thus giving body and life to all the rest." At last, he writes, he invites the reader to "rest his mind" as his own is resting.[12]

While it is true that Wordsworth does not discuss in this passage or the one on "To Joanna" any of the poems that concern us, he does provide a sense of the voice found in the poems written between the two commentaries. Unlike the voice, distant and undefined, that appears in the ballads written early in the year 1802, this voice is based upon the power of the images called up by the mind to "trap" the mind in its journey from rest through surprise to delight, and finally back to rest. It is occupied with serious concerns but approaches them with lightness; it "wantons with grateful joy" and with "mingled allusions suffused with humor." It displays a flexibility and technical variety newly learned by the poet and often skillfully applied and opens the way to complex and highly successful experiments with traditional forms in two related but quite different poems, "Resolution and Independence" and the "Immortality Ode." Our task now is to examine the lyric verse of that "sweet spring the best-beloved & best" ("A Farewell," line 50) in the light of these remarks.

BIBLIOGRAPHICAL NOTE

My effort to define a characteristic Wordsworthian voice has its precedents. But others who have discussed Wordsworth's several "voices" have often done so in order to separate his bad from

[12] *PW*, 3:18; *MY*, 2:148, 149. See Hartman, *The Unmediated Vision: An Interpretation of Wordsworth, Hopkins, Rilke, and Valéry* (New Haven, 1954), pp. 8, 9, 14, 17, and notes 7 and 17.

his good poetry. Perhaps the most extreme example of recent attempts is F. W. Bateson's division of the Wordsworth canon into two "voices": on the one hand he finds "an essentially objective poetry, evincing a strong sense of social responsibility, but crude, naive and often bathetic" (this he calls the "Augustan manner"); on the other "an essentially subjective poetry, egocentric, sentimental and escapist, but often charming because of its spontaneity" (this is the "Romantic manner"). His conclusion, that "the great poems . . . are those which combine the two elements in Wordsworth's poetry in a new inclusive whole," is promising but less than demonstrable on his terms (*Wordsworth: A Re-Interpretation*, pp. 14, 15). He finds this to be the case in the "best passages" of *The Prelude*, the Lucy series, "Michael," "Resolution and Independence," and a few others. Albert S. Gérard argues convincingly for the last poem as a rare but brilliant instance in which the "voice of vision" and the "voice of fact" perfectly conjoin (" 'A Leading from Above': Wordsworth's 'Resolution and Independence,' " first published in 1960; revised and included in *English Romantic Poets* [Berkeley and Los Angeles, 1968]). My own discussion of that poem is meant to show more fully the evolution within the poem of these two voices.

Donald Davie, however, takes a literary and historical standpoint, rather than a psychological one, and claims that "Wordsworth was technically incompetent" until 1801, when he "put himself to school with Chaucer, Shakespeare and Milton." Before then he had "by luck or genius" used "primitive forms which could just sustain what he had to say." He goes on to acknowledge that the poet emerges, around 1802, after "some uncomfortable experiments," as an accomplished craftsman. "He creates not one style, but many, according to what he needs to do." The most important of the "styles" developed by the poet at this critical stage, according to Davie, are those of the political sonnets, *The Prelude*, and the "Immortality Ode." He does not consider the lyrics (*Purity of Diction in English Verse* [London, 1953], pp. 112, 113).

More subtle distinctions are made by David Perkins, who like Davie uses the more inclusive term, "style." Perkins finds that "at one extreme, the language tends to be simple, colloquial, and concrete," while at the other, "it becomes abstract, poly-syllabic, complexly articulated, copious, and even pleonastic." There are as well "two distinct activities of mind." The one, "description, observation, or narration," is connected with "homely language"; the other, "reflection or meditation," with "overt interpretation of concrete experience" in meditative or doctrinal passages. Perkins finds it possible to refine his comment by saying that "the verse that tells a story or incident is usually rather quiet in feeling," themes are understated or indirectly expressed, or "qualified by a sense of potential comedy," while strong emotion occurs primarily in meditation (*Wordsworth and the Poetry of Sincerity* [Cambridge, Mass., 1964], pp. 216, 317). His categories are not easily kept separate, however.

Finally, Alan Grob has noticed the appearance of "an important new Wordsworthian genre" in the spring of 1802: "the lyric apostrophe to nature's more familiar and common objects." He regards this new genre as "not merely a variation in form but also a significant contraction in Wordsworth's span of vision." In the remainder of his essay he attempts to distinguish between the themes and form of selected 1802 lyrics and those of the poet's earlier verse. But he is primarily interested in the philosophic content of these poems ("To a Butterfly"— both poems, "To a Cuckoo," and "My heart leaps up") as they stand in relation to the "Immortality Ode" ("Wordsworth's 'Immortality Ode' and the Search for Identity," *ELH* 32 [1965]: 33 and *passim*).

[3]
The Patterned Past:
Experiments in Symbolic Form

What then are the elements of this lyric voice? First, the lightly turning mind contemplates significance in apparent triviality. But beneath this process, and often helping to bring it about, is Wordsworth's memory. The poet's central theme and mode, the workings of memory, provide the most characteristic structure of the poems spoken in this voice. It need not be stressed how memory, with its rich variety of form, content, and emotional effect, pervades the work of the poet, especially in the years 1797–1807. The spring of 1802 brought a crisis of memory for Wordsworth. He had been balked in his efforts to continue *The Prelude* and the rest of *The Recluse*. The feelings of continuity provided by Dorothy in a personal sense and by Coleridge in a philosophical sense seemed seriously endangered, the latter by Coleridge's growing illness and the early signs of his estrangement and the former by Wordsworth's impending marriage.[1]

---

[1] Dorothy's role in her brother's "recovery" is much disputed. Wordsworth discusses her effect upon him in *An Evening Walk, PW*, 1:12, *app. crit.;* "Lines composed a Few Miles above Tintern Abbey," *PW*, 2:262, 263, ll. 111–159; "Home at Grasmere," *PW*, 5:313ff.; and *Prel*, 6:208–218; 10:908–921; 11:196–224; 13:211–246. As will be seen

As we shall see, the poetry of this period in large measure
bears out this deep concern for continuity.

Many have noticed an apparent contradiction in Wordsworth's use of memory, one especially evident during the period in question. Wordsworth takes pleasure in regret; out
of yearning he recreates images of the past, yet in his "philosophic mind" accepts their having gone; he admits the moment has passed, yet insists it will remain. He wrote in 1800,

> I look into past times as prophets look
> Into futurity a [?thread ?trail] of life runs back
> Into dead years, the [?faculty ?fantasy] of thought
> The lyric spirit of philosophy
> Leads me through moods of sadness to [?and] delight.[2]

Peculiarly Wordsworthian paradoxes are concentrated into
these few lines: "past times / futurity," "thread of life /
dead years," "sadness / delight." Under scrutiny, however,
the contradictions became meaningful paradox, a deliberate
attempt to probe beneath the obvious. This paradox is
crucial to the difficult structure of the "Immortality Ode,"
as we shall see in the final chapter, but it is the basis as well
for a characteristic design in the lyrics of the spring of 1802,
a design of recovery.

Three basic types emerge from the group. There are narrative lyrics, like "Among all lovely things," a poem strongly

---

from the discussion below, in the spring of 1802 she is often at the
very center of her brother's "evocations of the personal past." Coleridge's philosophical quest for "continuity" hardly needs documenta-
tion, but see *STCNB* 1:556, 921.

2 DCP, MS Verse 42 (interleaved copy of Coleridge's *Poems*, 1796),
used by Wordsworth in an early stage of the composition of "Michael."
See *PW*, 2:480, for de Selincourt's transcription; his is not an ac-
curate copy, however. Karen Green has helped me in deciphering
these difficult lines.

reminiscent of the Lucy elegies (especially "Strange fits of passion"), and like "Foresight," a poem linked to the lyrical ballads "We are Seven" and "Lucy Gray." There are descriptive lyrics, often with an extemporaneous quality, like "Written in March," a rare kind of poem for Wordsworth, who remarks in *The Prelude* how unlike him it is "to make / A present joy the matter of [his] Song" (1:55–56). And there are reflexive lyrics like "To a Cuckoo." [3] This last form is most common to the short poems. Of the sixteen in this group several share a specific pattern, one based on a technique Wordsworth himself conceived of as double consciousness. [4] In this pattern the present confronts the past, and in the best of these poems the both-and relation between now and then, regret and joy, is the means to achieving the permanence that Wordsworth sought in the mundane. Wordsworth writes, early in the second book of *The Prelude,* in a passage composed in early 1800:

A tranquillizing spirit presses now
On my corporeal frame: so wide appears

[3] There are, too, the creative adaptations like the "Spenserian" valedictory, "A Farewell," and the Thomsonian "Stanzas." He also finished some blank-verse lyrics he had begun earlier: "This is the spot" and "When to the attractions of the busy world."

[4] M. H. Abrams has recently called attention to the special meditational form in which Wordsworth actually revisits a scene, thus doubly exposing it to the "quiet eye" ("Poet's Epitaph"): "The two landscapes fail to match, and so set a problem ('a sad perplexity') which compels the meditation." He adapts Wordsworth's phrase, "two consciousnesses," to designate "the wonderfully functional device" ("Structure and Style in the Greater Romantic Lyric," in *From Sensibility to Romanticism,* p. 533). But as I argue below, Wordsworth meant the phrase in a broader, more inclusive, sense. For though meditation is often implied within or beyond the frame of the poem it is rarely expressed overtly in the short poem of this type (see Perkins, *Wordsworth and the Poetry of Sincerity,* p. 193).

The vacancy between me and those days,
Which yet have such self-presence in my mind
That, sometimes, when I think of them, I seem
Two consciousnesses, conscious of myself
And of some other Being. [2:27–33]

More than in emotion recollected in tranquillity, poetry is generated in the poet's discovery of himself as both onlooker and participant, and in the need, simultaneously raised, to make them one, or as Coleridge put it, to identify "the percipient and the perceived." [5] The pattern evolved by the poet to express this relationship between the redeemed observer and the still struggling wayfarer, this new-man–old-man paradox, while not restricted to the lyrics of 1802, of course, is indigenous to them and has there its own clarity and balance.

In the first of the two poems "To a Butterfly," despite a plainness of syntax that borders on parataxis, the basic contrast between stillness and flight is established in the first line and echoed again in lines two and five. The next lines,

Much reading do I find in thee;
Thou Bible of my infancy! [3–4]

connect present to past by means of the Butterfly, who, like the divinely given Bible, not only renders the past meaningful to the present but promises a meaningful future as well. This sense is lost in the revision, where the Butterfly becomes a "Historian" of the poet's infancy with whom he holds "converse." Significantly, the poet settles on the "historian" figure, which emphasizes the pastness, the irrevocable nature of memory, while the original trope suggests its revivifying power. In any case, dead times, the solemn image of his "Father's family," are revived by the "gay Creature."

5 *STCNB*, 1:921 [1801].

In the second stanza, having successfully mingled past with present, solemnity with gaiety, the poet slips into a joyous memory, itself structured by contrast, of aggressive brother with gentle sister in pursuit of butterflies. The momentary Butterfly, its momentariness suggestive of both its brief stay in the poet's view and its short life on earth, calls back two images, then. One image, "solemn" and only named, is a brief image in precisely that double sense in which the Butterfly's stay is brief: the thought is truncated, and Father is dead. The other image, "gay" and fully drawn, is an apparently timeless vision of the two children. It is timeless, despite the past tense, because of its vividness and its power to reach, via the present Butterfly, over the now collapsed years ("the days / The time") into the present "moment."

This method is extended into the second Butterfly poem. Here the contrast, similar to the one in the first poem, is drawn between the still Butterfly and the stirring breeze. The poet dwells upon and expands the apparent contradiction:

> I know not if you sleep or feed
> How motionless! not frozen seas
> More motionless. [4–6]

Rather like the "Bible" figure of the first poem, the usually restless but now motionless sea is almost (perhaps purposely) too large a metaphor for its humble referent. The breeze, not yet come, will bring the corresponding "joy" of motion. That marvelous stasis achieved by the Butterfly, however, suggests to the poet a twofold scene, one within the other. In stanza two he offers the Butterfly a timeless sanctuary in which to feed at peace, free of change, and to "converse" with the poet and his sister-companion, the keepers of this orchard-garden paradise; but once there, another older paradise will supplant the present one, at least in memory.

> We'll talk of sunshine and of song
> And summer days when we were young
> Sweet childish days that were as long
> As twenty days are now. [16–19]

There is a certain playful "wishfulness" here, just as there is in the first Butterfly poem an element of mild self-mockery, but the pattern is characteristic.

"The Sparrow's Nest" develops the pattern further by a series of transitions in time that eventually overcome time. The poem begins in the present:

> Look! five blue eggs are gleaming there
> Few visions have I seen more fair
> Nor many prospects of delight
> More pleasing than this simple sight. [1–4]

The movement of the past happens with a "start" as an image of another sparrow's nest comes unsummoned by Bible or Historian. Significantly, the tense shifts with the scene and the mood: "I started," the poet says, even though he has just enjoined us to "look" now. The scene expands, as in the second Butterfly poem, to include his sister, and in stanza two the poet shifts the focal center to her:

> She look'd at it as if she fear'd it
> Still wishing dreading to be near it
> Such heart was in her, being then
> A little Prattler among men. [11–14]

In the last six lines we return to the poet in the present who pays tribute to the gifts his sister has made him. The doubt raised by the final lines as to whether the gifts were received in the time of the central vision of the poem or in the "later years" of line 15, may suggest the continuous nature of the memory. There are to be sure two "poets" and an inkling of a third: the first vision (1–4) calls up a second (5–14) which, as the poet recollects, startled him; the second vision gives way to a middle ground, "blessing of my later years," which in turn shades into the altered present, with the poet enumerating the sisterly gifts (15–20).

In "To a Cuckoo," perhaps the clearest example of the technique, "then" touches "now" as in the first three poems, but the form is here under masterful control.

> O blithe new-comer I have heard
> I hear thee and rejoice: [1–2]

The tense change contains in it the kernel of the poet's effort to conquer time. In "The Sparrow's Nest" Wordsworth had barely hinted at his meaning through this device: here it is used to perfection. The shifts of time represented in the tense change are sustained and expanded in the poem so that time itself widens. The simple device doubles ("beget[s] again," st. VII) the vision; it corresponds to, is almost an "image" of, the poet's internal response.[6]

But when was the sound heard? in the distant past, the recent past, the present, or all three? Without answers, one riddle follows another:

> O cuckoo shall I call thee bird
> Or but a wandering voice? [3–4]

The next lines, which remain in the present tense, seem to solve the puzzle of lines three and four:

> While I am lying on the grass
> I hear thy hollow shout

[6] See Hartman, *Wordsworth's Poetry*, p. 270. Schachtel calls this kind of experience a "resensation": "By revival of a former sensation

47

From hill to hill it seems to pass
About & all about. [5–8]

The shout is "hollow" (wanting body, sepulchral) [7] and appears to "wander" from hill to hill. But the third stanza presses further the distinction between "bird" and "voice":

To me no Babbler with a tale
Of sunshine and of showers
Thou tellest Cuckoo in the vale
Of visionary hours. [9–12]

Here, the poet deliberately rejects the trivial and "adult" or commonsense response to the "bird" as "Babbler with a tale / Of sunshine and of showers"; he turns instead to "the visionary hours" called up by the voice. Stanza four is a second invocation, for now the dichotomy suggested in stanza one becomes clear:

Thrice welcome, darling of the spring!
Ev'n yet thou art to me
No Bird, but an invisible thing,
A voice, a mystery. [13–16]

The voice, once "heard" in line 1, is the voice of mystery; while the voice being heard (line 2) is in danger of descending to that of a mere "bird," a "Babbler" to the complacent and spritually atrophied listener. But the voice, both heard once and now being heard, through the agency of memory, becomes

The same who in my school-boy days
I listen'd to, whom I

___

the attitude of the former self that first had this sensation is remobilized" (in *Metamorphosis,* p. 312).

7 *OED.* The revisions to "restless" and "loud note" are less expressive; the final change to "two-fold" is perhaps the best, amplifying as it does the double nature of the voice.

> Look'd for a thousand thousand ways
> In bush, and tree, & sky.[8]

It is indeed "thrice welcome"—welcome then, now, and in times to come.

And the poet's voice, like the bird's voice, shifts back in time:

> To seek thee did I often rove
> Through woods & on the green
> And thou wert still a hope a love
> Still long'd for never seen. [21–24]

The last stanzas return to the present moment, with the poet still aware of the "vacancy between [him] and those days" (*Prel,* 2:29); but capable now, through the office of the bird's unifying voice, of begetting "that golden time again." The "mystery" of stanza four is revived and given a "place" on the ordinary "earth" paced by men, "an unsubstantial fairy place," the "fit home" for both the poet, who is now in touch with his past self, and the bird. Like the two voices, child and man are "the same."

This structure, based on a recovery of the past, is found in two of the longer poems of the period as well. In the "Immortality Ode" the form and content of memory fuse; as in "To a Cuckoo," memory of sound and sight in the past shapes the experience of the present. "Resolution and Independence" begins with that same trick of memory found in "To a Cuckoo," the shifting of tense, and contains the device of placing scenes within scenes within the mind; it records one of those "spots of time" that take on meanings during the very process of recollection. But the perfection of the form as developed here is to be found in two lyrics

[8] Lines 17–20. The hyperbole is softened by revision: "that Cry / Which made me look a thousand ways."

written about the time Wordsworth was working at white heat on *The Prelude* (1804–1805)—"I wandered lonely as a cloud" and "The Solitary Reaper." In each poem there is the familiar lapse of time between the incident and the recording of that incident in the lyric voice; each is shaped by the memory evoked, for in each the characteristic pattern described above is developed to a point of great economy and suppleness. The second poem, based, like the Cuckoo poem, on sound rather than sight, ends,

> I listen'd till I had my fill:
> And, as I mounted up the hill,
> The music in my heart I bore,
> Long after it was heard no more.[9]

In the short poems of 1802, even in those which appear to be *extempore,* the poet slips back in time, seeks roots in the past wherever they can be found. The first Daisy poem begins in the turbulent past in order to reach forward to the "delights" of the present. The poem "The Green Linnet" hovers strangely between past and present just as the bird seems to "hover" among the hazel trees (25–28). The last stanza divides evenly, four lines in the present, four in the past tense:

> While thus before my eyes he gleam*s*
> A Brother of the leaves he seem*s*
> When in a moment forth he teem*s*
> His little song in gushes;

[9] "The Solitary Reaper," quoted from the 1807 version, 29–32, *Wordsworth's Poems in Two Volumes* (Oxford, rev. 2d ed. 1951), ed. Helen Darbishire, p. 187. The effect is even clearer in the revised version of line 29: "I listened motionless and still" (*PW*, 3:77). Schachtel orders the senses along a scale from "distance" (highly intellectual) to "proximity" (non-intellectual), from sight to touch. Hearing is one step closer to "proximity" than sight (pp. 298, 299).

As if it pleas'd him to disdain
And mock the form which he *did* feign,
While he *was* dancing with the train
Of Leaves among the bushes. [33–40]

Though the poet may have needed the forms of the past
tense to eke out the meter, the "as if" construction does not
demand those forms. In any case, the effect is the same. The
jaunty song, beginning "The cock is crowing," is titled in
manuscript as follows: "Written while resting on the Bridge
near the foot of Brother's Water, between one & two o'clock
at noon April 16, 1802." The title's elaborate specificity is
not unlike that of titles for epigrams in the *Greek Anthology*
and for later inscriptions and epitaphs by eighteenth-century
English poets, and by Wordsworth himself. The lyric response of the poem is thus given roots in the milieu of its
inspiration, which is, in a way, a means of giving it a past
and insuring it a future as an enduring "spot of time." [10]

Related to these efforts to root present experiences in
memory, but different in kind from the poems of recovery,
the poems of "discovery" deal with naked objects, uncon-
nected with the past. The unpretentious "lesser" Celandine,
the ubiquitous but unprepossessing Daisy, the Barberry
Tree, the Sky-lark: these "pleasures newly found," the poet
says, "are sweet" ("To the Same Flower" [Celandine]). In
these lyrics Wordsworth often seems to be stretching forward
in time, invoking the moment when these simplest objects

[10] See Hartman's essay "Wordsworth, Inscriptions, and Romantic
Nature Poetry," pp. 391, 408n. But see also Mayo, "Contemporaneity
of the *Lyrical Ballads*," pp. 492, 516. "Writers everywhere," Mayo reports, "had been seeking to give their works an air of spontaneity by
emphasizing their casual, extemporaneous qualities." One might also
cite the detailed notes on the "origins" of his poems which Wordsworth dictated to Isabel Fenwick in his old age.

will also have the power to restore. The two Celandine poems attempt for this flower what other poets have done for "Pansies, lilies, kingcups, daisies." A flower unnoticed by the poet "thirty years and more" (21), only now does she win appropriate greeting (23–24). Playfully self-conscious of the role of spokesman, the poet chides other poets for ignoring her, and scolds other flowers for pre-empting her glory. The final stanza of the first Celandine poem looks determindedly and seriously forward to future songs:

> Prophet of delight and mirth
> Scorn'd and slighted upon earth
> Herald of a mighty band
> Of a joyous train ensuing
> Singing at my heart's command
> In the lanes my thoughts pursuing
> I will sing as doth behove
> Hymns in praise of what I love.[11]

The line, "singing at my heart's command," is somewhat ambiguous; but it can mean that, metaphorically, the poet's heart will command (through memory) all the mighty band of joyous singers (birds and flowers perhaps) heralded by their forerunner, the Celandine. Hope of future recollection in turn calls from the poet a promise of songs in praise of what he loves. In the second Celandine poem, probably an overflow from the first, the speaker turns to scold himself for his ignorance of the flower before him, "Yet, I long could overlook / Thy bright coronet," and his ignorance as well of the literary tradition, "thy store of other praise." With his

11 Lines 57–64. Greater seriousness is gained, as well as a certain remoteness, by a later revision (1836) at lines 61–62: "Serving at my heart's command / Tasks that are no tasks renewing." The revision does not clarify the ambiguous syntax.

eye on the future, then, the poet supplies his own praise of the humble monument,

> Build who will a pyramid
> Praise it is enough for me
> If there are but three or four
> Who will love my little flower. [45–48]

The first Daisy poem is another hymn of praise, addressed to that "milder day," which is both the Daisy's habitat and an apt metaphor for the state of mind that the Daisy induces in the mature poet:

> When stately passions in me burn
> If some chance look to thee should turn
> I drink out of an humbler urn
> A lowlier pleasure. [57–60]

The mind made quiet by the chance look opposes both the early "appetitive" phase described in the opening stanza,

> In youth from rock to rock I went
> From hill to hill in discontent
> Of pleasure high and turbulent
> Most pleas'd when most uneasy, [1–4]

and the "stately passions" of the present moment. The poet's debt for this "happy genial influence" (70) is repaid in the final lines by a prophecy of his own:

> Thou long the Poet's praise shalt gain;
> Thou wilt be more belov'd by men
> In times to come: thou not in vain
> Art nature's favorite. [77–80]

In the third Daisy poem the flower is praised for its "function apostolical / In peace fulfilling" (23–24), in the second ("With little here to do or see") for its gift of gladness and meekness (46–48), but in each case with reference to the flower's immediate regenerative, almost "tranquillizing," effect, and not to its link with the poet's other "consciousnesses," except through future recollection.

In "These chairs they have no words to utter," a curious poem in two parts never printed by the poet, this tranquillized state is explored by means of an unusual before-and-after structure. Although the poem is spoken in the present, it contains its own past and future. The speaker muses without aid of memory as his eye falls only upon a few silent chairs and other inert objects in the room; he relies instead upon the contrast between two states of mind, or rather the same state (tranquillity) modified by the passage of "half an hour." The first two stanzas evoke and seek to maintain a solitary death-like peace; the last two reject the loneliness of death itself, suggested by its surrogate in the second stanza, "Happy as they who are dead" (12). Rather the poet would have a "deep delicious peace" which will keep "the quiet of death" but maintain as well the "sweetness and breath" of life and companionship: "Yet be thou ever as now. . . . Peace, peace, peace" (28–30). The poem is, in effect, a wish for an eternal present.[12]

In "To a Skylark" the poet makes every human effort to join the bird, almost, it would seem, in a physical sense:

[12] Alan Grob treats it as two poems (following de Selincourt's publication of them as "Fragments" [*PW*, 4:365], perhaps). The first "fragment" is the one clear occasion in which Wordsworth's own voice speaks hopefully of death; in the second he reverses his judgment and realizes that "to die is not to purify life of encumbrance and distraction and thereby to intensify its richness," but rather to "repose in nullity" ("Wordsworth's 'Immortality Ode' and the Search for Identity," p. 49). But by dividing the poem sharply into two fragments, Grob misses the fact that the second part transforms rather than reverses the attitude of the first. It is a unified poem of considerable interest and power.

> Up with me, up with me into the clouds!
>   Singing, singing
> With all the clouds about us ringing,
>   We two will sail along.[13]

He begins in weariness, a familiar Wordsworthian pattern,
but ends, despite the efforts to soar, in resigned cheerfulness,
having failed to reach the lark's delirious heights:

> Hearing thee or else some other
>   As merry a brother,
> I on earth will go plodding on
> By myself chearfully till the day is done.   [28–31]

More impressive in its way than any of these last few
poems, "The Barberry Tree" closes on a note reminiscent
of the ending of "Tintern Abbey" (134–159). The poet says
to his companion, whom he has urged to witness the *berberis*
as he has done:

> And then like me
> Ev'n from the blossoms of the Barberry,
>   Mayst thou a store of thought lay by
> For present time and long futurity:
>   And teach to fellow-men a lore
>   They never learn'd before;
> The manly strain of nat'ral poesy.[14]

[13] Lines 3–6. Much of this effect is toned down or "naturalized" in
later revisions, even before Coleridge's public strictures against the
poem in *BL*. Compare with lines 5–6, "With all the heav'ns about
thee ringing, / Lift me, guide me, till I find / That spot which seems so
to thy mind" (1807). And "I have sung in wildernesses dreary" becomes
"I have walk'd through wildernesses dreary" (7). But Wordsworth
himself is unconvinced by the patch job done in 1827 and must apolo-
gize for an even heavier-footed closing stanza than the first attempt.
See *PW*, 2:510–511.

[14] Lines 107–113. See Jonathan Wordsworth, "The New Wordsworth
Poem," *College English* 27 (1966): 455–465. He notes parallels with the

Finally, there is one poem that brings all these threads of design together to weave its own comprehensive but distinctive pattern:

> My heart leaps up when I behold
> A Rainbow in the sky:
> So was it when my life began;
> So is it, now I am a man,
> So be it, when I shall grow old
> Or let me die!
> The Child is Father of the man;
> And I should wish that all my days may be
> Bound each to each by natural Piety.

Past, present, and future here meet in the double image of leaping heart and arching rainbow in the first two lines. The next three lines spell out the stages from child, to man, to old man in discursive fashion, but are punctuated by the plea for death should the living memory of the rainbow "die" (7). The last three lines offer paradox and prayer much in the spirit of the New Testament and the Psalm. "The child is Father of the man" sounds like a naturalized version of New Testament old-man–new-man wisdom. The last two lines strongly suggest the language and spirit of the reflective Psalms, like Psalm 90 in which the singer reiterates his sense of the daily threat of "separation" (we are "soon cut off"), and asks, "So teach us to number our days, that we may apply our hearts unto wisdom" (12): "O satisfy us early with thy mercy; that we may rejoice and be glad all our days" (14). These vague allusions serve a function similar to that of metaphor and symbol by spreading the field of reference beyond the literal statement of the lines. The far-

---

Daffodil poem, the "Immortality Ode," and "The Solitary Reaper" (p. 459).

reaching implications of Wordsworth's "psalm," structured as it is upon the unbroken progress of "rememberable life,"[15] open the way to the deep concerns and darker notes of the two long poems of the period, "Resolution and Independence" and the "Immortality Ode."

BIBLIOGRAPHICAL NOTE

Studies of memory in Wordsworth's verse were no doubt initiated by the perceptive Hazlitt when he wrote that "every object" in his poetry "is seen through the medium of innumerable recollections" (*Complete Works*, 4:112). Bennett Weaver has discussed its function in *The Prelude* in "Wordsworth's 'Prelude': An Intimation of Certain Problems in Criticism," *SP* 31 (1934): 534–540, and "Wordsworth's 'Prelude': The Poetic Function of Memory," *SP* 34 (1937): 552–563. Many critics have touched upon it, but recently Christopher Salvesen in *The Landscape of Memory* (London, 1966) has "tried to suggest that the workings of memory provide a useful and illuminating 'way in' to much of Wordsworth's best poetry; and that memory—in literature a comparatively new mode of experience—is closely involved in Wordsworth's originality, in his poetic development, in his historical position, and in his own feelings (and those of his age) about time, landscape, and autobiography, the evocation of the personal past" (from the Preface, p. v). Biographers and others have long speculated, too, on the reasons for Wordsworth's use of memory, the exact nature of its restorative power, and his need for the personal continuity it seemed to provide. For a convenient summary (though a selective one) see Hartman, *Wordsworth's Poetry*, pp. 381–382; and for further comment see Hartman's own concern with this problem in his book, *passim*, but

[15] Wordsworth's pencil note in MS M, beside the text of the poem. See also MS JJ of the *Prelude*, "the time [years] of unrememerable being" (*Prel*, p. 633).

especially chapters 6 and 7. The best brief study of memory of the Wordsworthian kind is by Ernest G. Schachtel, "On Memory and Childhood Amnesia" (1947; reprinted in his *Metamorphosis: On the Development of Affect, Perception, Attention, and Memory* [New York: Basic Books, 1959], pp. 279–322). Schachtel considers "the causes of the forgetting of early childhood and other trans-schematic experience [e.g., dreams]" and investigates how "a scene from childhood, buried under layers of years of a conventional life, reappears as though it had been yesterday" (309). Because "lost" memories do not fit into the scheme of conscious rationality, they come to us, he argues, with a certain strangeness about them. And because they come apparently from a world without schemes, divisions, and categories, these "involuntary memories" give a sense of wholeness. "Each genuine recovery of forgotten experience and, with it, something of the person that one was when having the experience carries with it an element of enrichment, adds to the light of consciousness, and thus widens the conscious scope of one's life" (311). For two recent studies of the function of memory in the "Immortality Ode" see below, Chapter 7, note 1.

[4]
Words and the Incarnation of Thought: Experiments in Symbolic Language

As Wordsworth moved toward a strong sense of form in the short lyric and as he advanced in the language of vision, he also developed a high degree of technical facility. To show his growing mastery of technique and to reveal the part it plays in defining the characteristic voice of this period, we need to examine the poet's metrical experiments as well as his uses of language. But first, language.

"If words be not . . . an incarnation of the thought, but only a clothing for it, then surely will they prove an ill gift." So Wordsworth wrote in 1810.[1] He was no doubt thinking of Pope's couplet in the *Essay on Criticism:*

> True Wit is Nature to advantage dressed,
> What oft was thought, but ne'er so well expressed.

But he regarded his own poetic language as no less "precise"[2] than that of other poets; in fact, more so. The issue of language or "poetic diction," as he was given to call lan-

---

[1] *LCW*, 125.

[2] *MY*, 2:194; to Sir George Beaumont (February 1808). Wordsworth chides the inattentiveness of Sir George's friend in a misreading of "I wandered lonely as a cloud."

guage that he disapproved of, was much in his thoughts during this spring as he worked on the additions and supplement to the Preface to *Lyrical Ballads*. But his early, and somewhat aggressive, preference for the "language of conversation in the middle and lower classes of society" had been modified in the first Preface (1800) to "a selection of the real language of men in a state of vivid sensation." This bid for a plain style was tempered yet again by a passage added to the Preface in 1802:

If the Poet's subject be judiciously chosen, it will naturally, and upon fit occasion, lead him to passions the language of which, if selected truly and judiciously, must necessarily be dignified and variegated, and alive with metaphors and figures. I forbear to speak of an incongruity which would shock the intelligent Reader, should the Poet interweave any foreign splendour of his own with that which the passion naturally suggests: it is sufficient to say that such addition is unnecessary. And surely, it is more probable that those passages, which with propriety abound with metaphors and figures, will have their due effect, if, upon other occasions where the passions are of a milder character, the style also be subdued and temperate.[3]

It is true, of course, that what he gives rather reluctantly here he takes away in the Appendix on "Poetic Diction"; but in the Appendix the argument is designed as an especially strong antidote to what Wordsworth regarded as the dangerously swollen language, the "gaudiness and inane phraseology of many modern writers." [4]

Wordsworth's theory of poetic diction and the "real lan-

[3] "Advertisement" to *Lyrical Ballads* (1798), *LCW*, 10; Preface to *Lyrical Ballads* (1800), *LCW*, 16; (1802), *LCW*, 47–48. See W. J. B. Owen, *Wordsworth as Critic* (Univ. of Toronto Press: Toronto, 1969), 'The Additions of 1802," pp. 57–109, for a discussion of these changes.
[4] "Advertisement" to *Lyrical Ballads* (1798), *LCW*, 10.

guage of men" has caused much controversy and confusion, in his own time and in ours. But Coleridge, one of many to object to Wordsworth's argument, never ceased to link the style of the best of Wordsworth's poems with the plain or "neutral" style, a universal English which he associated particularly with the poetry of Samuel Daniel, Michael Drayton, and Sir John Davies. Coleridge writes in the *Biographia Literaria* that he finds in Wordsworth's verse "an austere purity of language both grammatically and logically; in short a perfect appropriateness of the words to the meaning." In this quality Wordsworth "strikingly resembles Samuel Daniel," a writer "whose diction bears no mark of time, no distinction of age." Though he thinks the opposing epithets, "well-languaged Daniel" and "prosaic Daniel," are apt, he admires that "style which, as the *neutral ground* of prose and verse, is common to both." [5]

There is little Elizabethan grace in the "ballads" of *Lyrical Ballads,* though they contain much of Daniel's or Drayton's plainness. Speaking of Wordsworth's ballads, Helen Darbishire aptly remarks, "Their language is as colorless as water." In these poems, she continues, " 'power' is introduced . . . into the world of literature . . . in its naked strength and simplicity." [6] Wordsworth knew, of course, as W. P. Ker has pointed out, that "imagination can use the

[5] 2:115, 119, 61. Coleridge made extensive notations in Lamb's copy of the 2d volume of Daniel's *Poetical Works,* in February 1808; they can be found in *Coleridge on the Seventeenth Century,* ed. Roberta F. Brinkley (Durham, N.C., 1955), pp. 509ff. Similar comments on Drayton with more on Daniel appear in Brinkley, pp. 508–509 (from *Table Talk,* dated 1831–1834); and on Davies, in *STCNB,* 2:2645 (August 1805).

[6] The term "power" appears in the 1800 Preface; Miss Darbishire's remarks are in her introduction to *Wordsworth, Poems in Two Volumes, 1807,* pp. xxxvii–xxxix.

simplest diction, because it has got at the truth, found what can appeal to the right mind of man, because it is strong in life, thought and language." [7] But he knew as well that the mind has other "moods," and it is just possible that he acquired a technique for expressing fanciful moods in unplain language from the authors with whom Coleridge and others so favorably compare him, many of whom he read with considerable care during the winter and spring, 1801–1802.[8] The diction, generally, in these poems shows a marked contrast with that of the *Lyrical Ballads*. One rather conservative estimate is that the latter are *"naked* poems" while the former are "less bare." Another critic goes much further by claiming that the "language is no longer 'the language spoken by men' but the richly reminiscent language of the poets. Spenser, Daniel, Ben Jonson, and above all Milton," it is said, "have given colour to his diction." However, one need only recall the spareness of "My heart leaps up," or be made aware of the "impression of utter simplicity, almost of artlessness" in the first Butterfly poem ("Stay near me"), or listen to the strict matter-of-factness of "The cock is crowing" in order to sense the extravagance of the latter claim. What does occur in the lyric poetry of 1802 is a gradual movement, corresponding to that found in "Resolution and Independence," from the bare elements of meter and con-

[7] *Form and Style in Poetry* (London, 1928), p. 250. He goes on to cite "such simple poems as Drayton's sonnet, 'Since there's no help, come, let us kiss and part,' and Herrick's lines, 'Now is the time when all the lights wax dim' "; these, he says, "are full of meaning, of stress, of 'passion'—to use Milton's term." Wordsworth's term was "power."

[8] See Curtis, "Wordsworth and English Poetry of the Sixteenth and Seventeenth Centuries," *Cornell Library Journal* 1(1966):28–39; and Abbie Findlay Potts, *The Elegiac Mode* (Ithaca, N.Y., 1967), pp. 67–150. William Heath in *Wordsworth and Coleridge* (pp. 23, 24, 124–127) speculates on possible influences from Wordsworth's readings in *British Poets*.

crete image to a chaste deployment of metaphor and symbol. And the concrete image itself begins to serve a wider, more "variegated" purpose. This "new" language, by no means a full return to the poets of the sixteenth and seventeenth centuries, is modern in its apparent privateness.[9] But, somewhat in the manner of Robert Herrick, George Herbert, and William Vaughan, Wordsworth permits the lightest elements of nature, phrased in the simplest elements of language, to carry the burden of reflection, often appearing to disguise the meditating mind, but fulfilling that mind's buried intent nevertheless. Especially in the matter of syntax does Wordsworth recall Herbert or Drayton, George Wither or William Browne: it is utterly simple and paratactic in most of the lyrics.

> The cock is crowing,
> The stream is flowing,
> The small birds twitter,
> The Lake doth glitter,
> The green field sleeps in the sun.
> ["Written while resting on the Bridge," 1–5]

> I have thoughts that are fed by the sun
> The things which I see
> Are welcome to me.
> ["These chairs they have no words to utter," 13–15]

The lightly punctuated manuscript lines raise few points of ambiguity, for in these poems the line, often the half-line,

---

[9] The critics cited are in the same order as in the text: Florence G. Marsh, *Wordsworth's Imagery: A Study in Poetic Vision* (Yale Studies in English, 121 [New Haven, 1952]), p. 20; Helen Darbishire, Introduction to *Wordsworth, Poems in Two Volumes,* p. xxxix; and Perkins, p. 179; see Perkins, p. 193, for a discussion of Wordsworth's "half-private language of imagery"; and R. A. Foakes, *The Romantic Assertion* (New Haven, 1958), pp. 34–35.

is Wordworth's natural unit of thought. Even in the relatively "ornate" poem, the "Immortality Ode" and "Resolution and Independence," the instances of syntactic elaboration are controlled and deliberately emphatic.

The effect of paratactic simplicity in the short lyrics, in contrast with more elaborate syntactic patterns in the long poems, is to support their straightforward appeal to common sights and sounds, to give them the limpid clarity they need to convey their beauty and singularity, finally their importance, to men:

> Look! five blue eggs are gleaming there
> Few visions have I seen more fair
> Nor many prospects of delight
> More pleasing than this simple sight.
>
> ["The Sparrow's Nest," 1–4]

A close study of the texts and variants of all the poems of 1802 reveals that as Wordsworth grew more conservative in his handling of poetic decorum he revised toward complexity of syntax, to some extent losing the harmony he had first achieved between simple image and simple language. However, in the edition of 1845 he frequently restored the earlier, simpler phrasing.[10]

Beyond syntax, we have seen Wordsworth object to the "foreign splendour" of imagery which does not arise out of the "passion" described, be it strong or mild. In the 1815 Preface he writes:

When the Imagination frames a comparison, if it does not strike on the first presentation, a sense of the truth of the likeness, from the moment that it is perceived, grows—and continues to

---

[10] This is especially obvious among the ballads. Notice, too, the highly sophisticated syntax of "The Affliction of Mary _____of_____" compared to "Alice Fell" or "The Sailor's Mother."

grow—upon the mind; resemblance depending less upon the outline of form and feature, than upon inherent and internal, properties:—moreover the images invariably modify each other.

And late in life he wrote, more pithily, "In lyric poetry the subject and simile should be as much as possible lost in each other." [11]

Sixteenth- and seventeenth-century poets often use the natural object as a text for "sermons" both courtly and moral, as in Robert Herrick's poem, "Upon Roses":

> Under a Lawne, then skyes more cleare,
> Some ruffled Roses nestling were:
> And snuggling there, they seem'd to lye
> As in a flowrie Nunnery:
> They blush'd, and look'd more fresh than flowers
> Quickned of late by Pearly showers.

These lines recall a segment of Wordsworth's second Daisy poem:

> A Nun demure of lowly port,
> Or sprightly Maiden of Love's Court,
> In thy simplicity the sport
> Of all temptations. [17–19]

But as Wordsworth brings "Love's court" to dress up the lowly daisy, Herrick offers the roses as compliment to Julia. He completes his poem:

> And all, because they were possest
> But of the heat of *Julia's* breast:
> Which as a warme, and moistned spring,
> Gave them their ever flourishing.

[11] *LCW*, 153; *LY*, 1:158–159, 16 November 1824; to Alaric Watts. Wordsworth did not rigidly distinguish between the terms "simile" and "metaphor" and often used either one to stand for the more general term "figure" or "trope."

A more sedate example from Herrick is his "Divination by a Daffadill":

> When a Daffadill I see,
> Hanging down his head t'wards me;
> Guesse I may, what I must be:
> First, I shall decline my head;
> Secondly, I shall be dead,
> Lastly, safely buryed.[12]

This poem, no doubt based on the epigrams upon natural objects found in the *Greek Anthology*, a tradition Wordsworth too was familiar with, sharply divides subject and simile. However, the best effects were achieved by bringing subject and image into closer accord, and in Herbert's "The Flower" the balance is beautifully maintained from beginning to end:

> How fresh, O Lord, how sweet and clean
> Are Thy returns! ev'n as the flow'rs in spring;
> To which, besides their own demean,
> The late-past frosts tributes of pleasure bring.
> Grief melts away
> Like snow in May,
> As if there were no such cold thing.
> Who would have thought my shrivel'd heart
> Could have recover'd greenness? It was gone
> Quite under ground; as flowers depart
> To see their mother-root, when they have blown;
> Where they together
> All the hard weather,
> Dead to the world, keep house unknown.[13]

---

[12] From "Hebrides," *The Poetical Works of Robert Herrick,* ed. L. C. Martin (Oxford, 1956), pp. 25, 38.

[13] From *The Temple,* in *The Works of George Herbert,* ed. F. E. Hutchinson (Oxford, 1953), pp. 165, 166, ll. 1–14.

Wordsworth does not often structure the poem by means of the single image, but in the second poem "To the Daisy," already referred to, he employs a design, the gathering up of a "web of similies," similar to that of Herbert's "Prayer I." [14] Like Herbert he relies upon the rich suggestiveness of such images to convey a subtle and far from simple meaning.

But what of the image as image? What is its origin and make-up, its quality and effect? In an early draft of lines 159–172 of Book VIII of *The Prelude* (p. 571), Wordsworth discusses at length the effects on the "heart" of "the common haunts of the green earth," later condensing this flurry of images into a few lines. He is preoccupied with the origins of "tenderness," the counter-emotion which accompanies those feelings of grandeur developed through "the ministry of fear." Tenderness, he says, comes "by admiration and by love . . . There doth our life begin" (3, 6). The passage forms a catalogue of images, those of light foremost among them, which includes nearly all of the main images of these spring lyrics: "water sparkling down a rocky slope . . . a beast . . . a bird . . . a flower . . . the rainbow . . . the cuckoo's shout . . . the glow-worm's faery lamp . . . the Skylark . . . a star" (16–51). Each one is an "amazement and a surprise of sense," which, "when it has pass'd away, returns again / In later days" (31–33). They are associated with past joy and, more particularly, with present renewal.

Wordsworth's "discoveries" (14) were many that spring: the glittering lake, and the blue sky with its sailing clouds ("The cock is crowing," 18–19), the ever present sunshine ("I've watched you now," 16; "These chairs . . .," 12, 21; "To the Lesser Celandine," 31; "In youth from rock to rock," 74;

[14] Herbert, *Works*, p. 51. See also the first poem ("Hopes what are they?——Beads of morning") of Wordsworth's "Inscriptions supposed to be found in and near a Hermit's Cell," *PW*, 4:202.

"Travelling," 1–2; "Stanzas," 16, 26; "A Farewell," 15, 17),
the "gleaming eggs" ("The Sparrow's Nest," 1), the "silver
Shield with boss of gold," ("With little here to do or say,"
30), the "glittering" rock ("A Farewell," 53–54), and the
"beautiful soft half moon" ("The Sun has long been set,"
13). All this brightness not yet fallen from the air is epitom-
ized in four lines of "To a Cuckoo":

> And I can listen to thee yet
> Can lie upon the plain
> And listen till I do beget
> That golden time again. [25–28]

The recurring epithet "golden" suggests the joy Wordsworth took in the various forms of light, for, he says, as "a
Boy I lov'd the sun" (*Prel*, 2:184). But of course he was not
the first to adopt it. Though it would be difficult to find a
time before this century when this ancient epithet was out of
favor, the Elizabethan poets were especially fond of it. "O
happy golden Age!" exclaims Daniel in "A Pastoral." The
sunny joy of Wordsworth's lyrics is common to much pastoral
verse of the sixteenth- and seventeenth-century poets. The
first eight lines of Daniel's "An Ode" suggest especially the
Daisy poems: "Now each creature joys the other" in "happy
days and hours," a bird sings in "silver showers" and the sun
is the "greatest torch of heaven." [15]
Occasionally there occurs what Earl Wasserman has called
the "spiritualizing" process in the contemplation of the
images of nature. "The object is perceived vividly," he
writes, "usually with great specificity; the husk is then dis-
solved; and when the phenomenon has at last become

[15] Both poems by Daniel are in Robert Anderson's *British Poets,*
4:225–226 (13 vols.; London, 1792–1795). Wordsworth owned and used
this set during the period under study.

'spiritualized' it passes into the core of the subjective intelligence." [16] This effect occurs in "The Green Linnet" where the bird is addressed as

> A Life, a Presence like the air,
> Scattering thy gladness without care. [21–22]

It is suggested, too, in "To a Skylark"—

> Had I now the soul of a Fairy
> Up to thee would I fly.
> There is madness about thee and joy divine
> In that song of thine [9–12]

and in the first poem "To the Daisy":

> I saw the[e] glittering from afar
> And here thou art a pretty Star
> Not quite so fair as many are
>   In heaven above thee
> Yet like a star with glittering breast
> Self-pois'd in air thou seem'st to rest. [25–30]

The best example, however, and one of those cited by Wasserman to support his argument, is in "To a Cuckoo":

> Thrice welcome, darling of the spring!
> Ev'n yet thou art to me
> No Bird, but an invisible thing,
> A voice, a mystery. [13–16]

But a further look into the poet's practice reveals that while there are a few clear examples which record the transition from "subject" to "simile," to use Wordsworth's archaic terms, or from image to symbol, the fusion he speaks of almost always takes place. The overrun garden and the

[16] "The English Romantics: The Grounds of Knowledge," *Studies in Romanticism* 4(1964) :25.

tumbled wall of "The Ruined Cottage" or the clipping tree and the unfinished sheepfold of "Michael" show Wordsworth's power to present an object in all its literalness yet urge it on the path toward symbol, making it seem to have arrived there of its own accord, by mere accretion and endurance.

His practice in the short poems of 1802 lies halfway between the expansive literalness of "Michael" and "The Ruined Cottage" on the one hand and on the other the densely packed imagery of the elegies written at Goslar in 1799, particularly the "Lucy" poems. Even in the latter group we note that only one of these, "A Slumber Did My Spirit Seal," attains to something like optimum compression. But in the lyrics of 1802 the journey from image to symbol is generally less dazzling than in the Lucy poems, yet more quick, sometimes more facile, than it is in the narrative poems mentioned. The scene itself is reduced, even miniaturized; the narrative, when there is one, is trimmed to the barest suggestion of story. The emphasis falls then on the images singled out, often repeated from poem to poem, often maintaining precarious balance, or compromise, perhaps, between expansiveness and density.

Under this new discipline the facile image of the "golden time" more often yields to the special place, the "spot," or bower, the secluded garden or "nook," where man and the creatures of Nature can find safety and peace. It is the "locus" for a blank verse lyric which Wordsworth probably worked on during this spring.[17]

17 It appears under the title "Travelling" in MSS SP (1802) and M (1804). Dorothy quotes it in *DWJ*, 157, 4 May 1802. The Wordsworths rarely missed an opportunity for making a bower (e.g., *DWJ*, 157, 6 May 1802) or for occupying a natural one. For other studies of the "bower" image, see Hartman, *Wordsworth's Poetry, passim,* and his "Wordsworth, Inscriptions, and Romantic Nature Poetry."

This is the spot:—how mildly does the Sun
Shine in between these fading leaves! the air
In the habitual silence of this wood
Is more than silent: and this bed of heath
Where shall we find so sweet a resting place?
Come!—let me see thee sink into a dream
Of quiet thoughts,—protracted till thine eye
Be calm as water, when the winds are gone
And no one can tell whither.—My sweet Friend!
We two have had such happy hours together
That my heart melts in me to think of it.

Here the bower is designated as the private "resting place" of the poet and his companion, without doubt his sister, where he can watch her "sink into a dream / Of quiet thoughts." In anticipation he pictures her eye transformed, like water on a windless day, calm and, presumably, reflecting the scene about her, forming an inner bower of the mind.[18] The poet's emotions as he witnesses this receding scene are, like those at the close of "Among all lovely things," inexpressible: his "heart melts . . . to think of it."

In the poem, "A Farewell," or "Our Departure" as it is called in Dorothy's *Journal* (p. 66), Wordsworth wrestles with the problem of introducing a third occupant into the "bower." The poem is ostensibly a leave-taking, but it expresses the almost desperate wish that time stand still, that the "easy-hearted" garden and its uneasy possessors may somehow remain at rest despite change:

[18] This implied meaning is perhaps encouraged by a later revision, "shutting up thyself within thyself." In another related passage he contrasts the immediate scene with the scene at large:

Come, thus invited, venture to exchange
The pomp of wide spread landscape for a mood
Of quiet thought.   [*PW*, 4:424]

Two burning months let summer over leap
And coming back with her who will be ours
Into thy bosom we again shall creep. [62–64]

The poem is a nostalgic review of the images of spring found in the other poems: [19] bright flowers, singing and nesting birds, "sunshine and shower" go to make up the "Dear Spot!" (33). The garden, too, we learn has "wayward" moods (42), is both "constant" and "fickle" (41). But despite its waywardness the poet asks that it

Help us to tell her tales of years gone by
And this sweet spring the best-beloved & best
Joy will be gone in its mortality,
Something must stay to tell us of the rest. [49–52]

What the "something" is that will compensate for lost joy is not made clear: the scene, perhaps, or the poetry inspired by it (cf. 55–56). But in any case, the poet pleads that his growing family's days be bound each to each, not merely his own. The circle of duty widens, but the doubt remains: will memory continue to vivify those days?

The bower is clearly described in the second Butterfly poem, again with Dorothy as co-occupant. It is implied as well in the other poems, often in interplay with the counter-image of a disrupted or fallen "paradise" (as in "The Redbreast and the Butterfly") or in subtle contrast to its natural opposite, the open spaces, often dangerous and threatening, where man "wanders," both physically and spiritually, in solitude. Wordsworth said of language, that, "if it do not uphold, and feed, and leave in quiet, like the power of gravitation or the air we breathe," then it "is a counter-spirit, unremittingly and noiselessly at work, to subvert, to lay

[19] It was written some time before May 31 even though the Wordsworths did not leave till July 9 (*DWJ*, 166, 189).

waste, to vitiate, and dissolve." [20] Though he speaks here in general terms about the poet's task, about the "benign conjunction" of "Reason and Passion," his words strike below the abstract issue to the power of words and the images they call up. Wordsworth as poet, if not as aesthetician, knew that poetry is no different from life: it has its spirits and its counter-spirits, its images and counter-images.

An obvious example of such a contrast appears in "To a Skylark," where the poet as earthbound "singer" is set against the free-souled bird:

> I have sung in wildernesses dreary;
> But today my heart is weary
> Had I now the soul of a Fairy
> Up to thee would I fly. [7–10]

But the same antithesis lies not far below the surface in "To a Cuckoo," the first "To a Butterfly" ("Stay near me") and many others. Thus the image of the bower implies what it strives to work against, placelessness: the physical homelessness of the wandering leech-gatherer, and the spiritual homelessness of the uneasy, restless poet in "Resolution and Independence" and especially in the "Immortality Ode":

> Turn wheresoe'er I may
> By night or day
> The things which I have seen I see them now no more.
> [7–9]

> But yet I know where'er I go
> That there hath pass'd away a glory from the earth.
> [17–18]

Another image and counter-image of equal interest and urgency is the happy child and the weary heart: on the one

[20] "Essay upon Epitaphs—III" (1810), *LCW*, 126.

hand there is Wordsworth's happy return to childhood or child-like response to the presences of nature and, on the other, his awareness of the unwanted but irreversible encroachments of the weary heart. Childhood or child-like experience is a theme central to several of the lyrics, often with a suggestion of its complement, a sense of deprivation or loss. Its finest expression comes in "To a Cuckoo" and stanzas I–IV of the "Ode." But Wordsworth's "effort to find in himself a continuing, unchanged identity, linking his adult self to his childhood," as one writer has put it,[21] can be traced in the two Butterfly poems, "The Sparrow's Nest," "The Green Linnet," and the first Daisy poem ("In youth from rock to rock"). It occurs also in two ballad-like poems, "Foresight" and "Among all lovely things." The first of these two last dramatizes an imagined childhood incident which Wordsworth based upon a blending of his own early experience and a chance remark by Dorothy. She had told him that when she was a child, she "would not have pulled a strawberry blossom."[22] The didactic title was added in 1804 and a final eight lines, rather heavily moralistic in tone, were appended in 1815. But the poem as it originally stood in 1802 is an attempt to recapture childhood responses to natural objects. "Among all lovely things," titled simply "The Glow-worm" in Dorothy's journal, is another, more successful, evocation of child-like response, this time speci-

[21] Perkins, p. 186.
[22] For his own experience see the sonnet appearing in Dorothy's letter of 6 May 1792 (EY, 1:74), "Sweet was the walk":

> And Childhood, seeming still more busy, took
> His little Rake; with cunning side-long look,
> Sauntering to pluck the Strawberries wild, unseen. [6–8]

Dorothy reports the conversation in DWJ, 151, 28 April 1802.

fically connected with the poet's sister. G. M. Harper has said that these "verses . . . belong among the mysterious 'Lucy poems.'"[23] But there is little mystery. The poem bears some resemblance to "Strange fits of passion have I known"; the two poems share a "homing" lover motif, and a structure that leads the reader to expect one kind of event or climax but gives him another. Each poem begins with a secret to be shared:

> Strange fits of passion have I known:
> And I will dare to tell,
> But in the Lover's ear alone,
> What to me befell.   [*PW*, 2:29, ll. 1–4]

> Among all lovely things my Love had been,
> Had noted well the stars, all flow'rs that grew
> About her home, but She had never seen
> A Glow-worm, never once—and this I knew.   [1–4]

The first poem ends not with an ordinary dramatic event but with a "fond and wayward" thought:

> "O mercy!" to myself I cried,
> "If Lucy should be dead!"   [27–28]

The second does close with an event, one that the speaker has elaborately prepared for, but it is collapsed or compressed into a single line:

> O joy it was for her and joy for me!   [20]

But the similarity between the two poems cannot be maintained for long. The Lucy poem does not give itself away in

[23] For the connection with Dorothy, see *EY*, 1:348, 16 April 1802; Emma or Emmeline is Wordsworth's poetic name for Dorothy. He did not reprint the poem after 1807. Harper's judgment appears in *William Wordsworth, His Life, Works, and Influence*, 3d ed. (London, 1929), p. 366.

the fourth line, as the later poem does. The earlier poem retains, even magnifies, its mystery by its conclusion, while "The Glow-worm" labors to dispel it. The iambic pentameter lines of "The Glow-worm" have an almost garrulous effect, so different from the delicate, chant-like compression of the ballad stanza in the Lucy poem. It is almost as if, burdened by the actual event, the poet could not escape its literalness.[24]

However, the poem has its own appropriateness. The prosaic "jogging" account of the preparation is followed by an admirably compressed and controlled response. The "stormy night," which has yielded the delicate glow-worm, gives way to a single moment of inexpressible joy, both for the initiate, Emma, and the "priest," who has prepared the "spot" and blessed the glow-worm "by name" with the same reverence summoned by his more orthodox counterpart in making ready a sacrament. The seriousness of the implied metaphor cannot be pressed, however, for the poem, in its mock-heroic account of the discovery of the glow-worm, maintains that mild self-deprecating tone found in the first Butterfly poem and elsewhere. But the tribute to Dorothy and the reverence for the final moment are genuine.[25] The intense moment of joy between "lovers," brought on by one of nature's tinier creatures, the child's reverence for the

[24] Dorothy tells how Wordsworth tried to write "Beggars" from her notes but found it impossible to "escape from those very words" (DWJ, 131, 13 March 1802).

[25] The theme of continuity is expressed in epigrammatic form by the single and quite flat, four-line stanza never printed by Wordsworth:

> I have been here in the Moon-light
> I have been here in the Day
> I have been here in the Dark Night
> And the stream was still roaring away.

"meanest flower," the sights and sounds of childhood that re-
surrect the "golden time," read singly, or grouped together
in this way, nevertheless imply their opposite too, the weary
heart, the waning or earthbound imagination.

The fear that his power to imagine and to create is falling off, or may soon subside, is also a dark undertone in
"To a Cuckoo" (25–32), "My heart leaps up" ("or let me
die"), "To a Sky-lark" ("I have sung in wildernesses dreary;
/ But today my heart is weary" [7–8]), and "To the Daisy":

> Is it that Man is soon deprest?
> A thoughtless Thing! who, once unblest,
> Does little on his memory rest
>   Or on his reason. ["Bright Flower," 9–12]

And, it might be argued, it underlies all the poems of "discovery" discussed above in which the poet appears to be out
in search of future memories.

Wordsworth said that as a child he "was often unable to
think of external things as having external existence." This
trait, or power as Wordsworth saw it, was one of the intimations of immortality he sought to sustain when upon him, to
recover when lost. All children are said to begin with this
"philosophy," by confusing "inner and outer, the psychic
and the physical," according to Jean Piaget, the eminent
Swiss child psychologist. At this stage, Piaget points out,
children do not "understand" metaphor, it is their way of
thought.[26] What little Wordsworth says about metaphor and
image, and his practice in poetry, suggest that he conceived
of the poet's task as the reenactment for the reader, who is
urged to follow the poet's lead, of this child-like sense of
singleness, the one life in all things, the "points" we all have
"within our souls, / Where all stand single" (*Prel,* 3:186–

---

[26] Jean Piaget, "Children's Philosophies," in *A Handbook of Child
Psychology* ed. Carl Murchison (Worcester, Mass., 1931), pp. 379–382.

187). About the Cuckoo poem he said that his "concise inter-
rogation" of the bird "dispossesses the creature almost of a
corporeal existence." [27] In the "almost" the cautious realist
speaks, but in the "dispossession" are the signs of an emerging symbolism. What Wordsworth achieves in the lyrics of
1802 generally is that delicate combination of a clear-sighted
actualism, a careful recording of images presented to the
quiet eye, with an adventurous illusionism, a fanciful pressing of language out toward the limits of verbal knowing,
toward symbol.

This dissolving of the object into symbol is linked to the
method of the two long poems. As we shall see, Wordsworth
makes powerful use of dream-like images in the revised
"Leech-Gatherer" (the rock-sea-beast-cloud metamorphosis,
and the figure of the pacing man); and later in the develop-
ing "Immortality Ode" he effects a brilliant return to the
"immortal sea,"

> And see the children sport upon the shore
> And hear the mighty waters rolling evermore.
>
> [164–165]

The special tone of the images in the lyrics consists in their
unusual lightness and joyousness, their clear notes of harmony, against a background of "lost joy" and solitariness.
The suggestion in the best lyrics ("To a Cuckoo," the two
Butterfly poems, "My heart leaps up") that the circle of
"celestial light" and harmony is getting smaller, as the light

[27] IF note to the "Immortality Ode," *PW*, 4:463; 1815 Preface, *LCW*,
148. The second passage is quoted by Moorman, 1:526; she then comments, "This is exactly what Wordsworth, by the alchemy of his
imagination, from his earliest boyhood had been doing with the world
of sense. He gazed on it until it 'revealed the invisible world' (*Prel*,
6:601 [1850])."

of common day closes in, is borne out by the "Immortality Ode" and "Resolution and Independence."

BIBLIOGRAPHICAL NOTE

The most interesting recent studies of Wordsworth's style in general have been Colin C. Clarke's *Romantic Paradox: An Essay on the Poetry of Wordsworth* (London, 1962), David Perkins' *Wordsworth and the Poetry of Sincerity* (Cambridge, Mass., 1964), and Hartman's *Wordsworth's Poetry* (New Haven, 1965). None has treated the 1802 poems exclusively.

[5]
Quaint Gaiety:
Learning to Sing

We have yet to make full account of the range of formal experimentation in the short lyrics. For in these shorter poems Wordsworth's touch is often light, even humorous. Furthermore his metrical variations are considerably more adventuresome than those in the *Lyrical Ballads*. His debt to the sixteenth- and seventeenth-century poets is not so specific or so thoroughgoing as some critics, Miss Darbishire, for example, would have it. Many phrases, she remarks, are "fathered by literary diction." But "more than this, the melody, the rhythm, the choice and order of the words are pervaded by the conception of sensuous beauty that thinks no shame to draw inspiration from the art of other poets." [1] Such a conception is hardly pervasive, though it is more true of "melody and rhythm," perhaps, than it is of diction. But beyond the few borrowed or "reminiscent" phrases that have been pointed out by various scholars, there are two important respects in which the voice of the spring lyrics comes very near the poetry of those "distinguished" poets of whom he was so fond: a humorous, playful, if not quite

[1] Introduction to *Wordsworth, Poems in Two Volumes*, p. xliv.

80

witty manner, and, for Wordsworth, an astonishing degree of metrical variety.[2]

Wordsworth's "humor" has been noticed before, usually for its scarcity or ineptitude. But John E. Jordan has argued for its real presence and strength. He finds that the poet's "most typical humor" is "a joyous parody of life." It is like caricature but lacks the strong satiric intention of that device. Rather "it comprehends a rich Hogarthian vision which sees life whole, realizes that it is not perfect, but finds it good." But Jordan, in making his best case for a "hearty masculine strain of humor," concentrates primarily upon the ballads and their comic extremes of characterization and description. Although the heartier, "vaguely Chaucerian," kind can be found in "The Tinker," written in April 1802, in the body of verse composed that spring there is a subtler and more quietly playful manner which is foreign to the *Lyrical Ballads,* and indeed to most of Wordsworth's poetry.[3]

The second Celandine poem contains a humorously incongruous, and quite Jacobean, yoking of tavern sign and flower:

> I have not a doubt but he
> Whosoe'er the man might be
> Who the first with pointed rays

[2] Southey detects "the best manner of old Wither" in the better "poemets" of these volumes (1807) (*The Life and Correspondence of the Late Robert Southey,* ed. Charles C. Southey [London, 1849–1850], 3:126); for specific parallels see the work of Hutchinson and Darbishire cited above; and Abbie F. Potts, "Spenserian and Miltonic Influence in Wordsworth's *Ode* and the *Rainbow,*" *Studies in Philology* 29 (1932): 607–616, and *The Elegiac Mode,* p. 67–172.

[3] "Wordsworth's Humor," *PMLA* 73 (1958): 86. This "significant strain of humor," however, all but dies out before the year 1806 (p. 93).

Workman worthy to be sainted
Set the sign-board in a blaze
When the risen sun he painted
Took the fancy from a glance
At thy glittering countenance. [9–16]

And in the second Butterfly poem there is the curious metaphor for the tiny butterfly resting quietly on a "yellow flower": "not frozen seas / More motionless" (5–6). The same wild exaggeration, used to praise a lady, not a flower, appears in the second stanza of Jonson's lyric "Her Triumph":

> Have you seene but a bright Lillie grow,
> Before rude hands have touch'd it?
> Have you mark'd but the fall o'the Snow
> Before the soyle hath smutch'd it?
> Have you felt the wooll o' the Bever?
> Or swan's down ever?
> Or have smelt o'the bud o'the Brier?
> Or the nard i' the fire?
> Or have tasted the bag o'the Bee?
> O so white! O so soft! O so sweet is she! [4]

Another example in Wordsworth's verse is found in the second Daisy poem where the poet weaves a "web of similies":

> And many a fond and idle name
> I give to thee, for praise or blame,

[4] From "A Celebration of Charis," *Underwoods* in *Ben Jonson: The Poems, The Prose Works*, ed. C. H. Herford and Percy and Evelyn Simpson, vol. 8, corr. ed. (Oxford, 1965), pp. 134–135, lines 21–30. The poem appears in *British Poets,* 4:562. Perkins notes that "as one potentially comic resource, Wordsworth possessed a habit of picturesque illustration by means of a bizarre image," p. 182.

As is the humour of the game,
While I am gazing. [13–16]

There follows a series of exuberant metaphors (not "similies")
for the flower: "Nun demur of lowly port . . . sprightly
Maiden of Love's Court . . . A Queen in crown of rubies
drest, / A Starvling in a scanty vest . . . A little Cyclops
. . . A silver Shield with boss of gold"; and finally, "When
all . . . reveries are past," it is simply "Sweet Flower!" As
we noted earlier, the design of the poem is remarkably like
Herbert's "Prayer I," in which he presents an array of images of different kinds and intensities: "Angels age" and
"Christ-side-piercing spear," "Heaven in ordinarie, man well
drest,"

> Church-bels beyond the starres heard, the souls bloud,
> The land of spices; something understood.[5]

Here as in Wordsworth's poem the pyrotechnical display
ends simply and quietly. Herrick's song "To Violets" also
has a form similar to that of the third Daisy poem: a journey
through playful hyperbole to the final "pointe" or turn:

> 1. Welcome Maids of Honour,
>   You doe bring
>   In the Spring;
>   And wait upon her.

> 2. She has Virgins many,
>   Fresh and faire;
>   Yet you are
>   More sweet then any.

> 3. Y'are the Maiden Posies,
>   And so grac't,

---

5 *Works*, p. 51.

To be plac't
'Fore Damask Roses.

4. Yet though thus respected,
    By and by
    Ye doe lie,
    Poore Girles, neglected.[6]

The difference, not one to be slighted, between these poems
and Wordsworth's "Daisy," lies in Herbert's ease in virtu-
osity, or in Wordsworth's conscious and leisurely stretching
after effects; in Herrick's compression—or in Wordsworth's
expansion—of the trivial. Herrick achieves epigrammatic
wit, without in the least revealing his feelings toward the
flowers, since that is not his intention; while Wordsworth
allows the poem to swell in an effort to express his feelings,
and, failing that, returns to the simplest expression, "Sweet
Flower!" But a playful, slightly mocking tone is essential
to the success of each.

Beyond this good-natured humor tempered by leisure, one
detects a gently satiric tone evident in some poems, often
taking the form of mild self-mockery, as in the poet's attitude toward his activities as a "very hunter" of butterflies,
pursuing them "with leaps and springs" ("Stay near me,"
12–16). This note occurs again in the disparity between the
exaggerated narrative and simple conclusion of "Among
all lovely things." And in "To the Lesser Celandine" he has
fun at the expense of "Poets, vain men in their mood," by
contrasting these "wanton wooers" with the "thrifty Cottager who stirs little out of doors" ("Pansies, lilies," 33–40),
but who "joys to spy" the small flower.

In a few poems the satire bites deeper. A mock-serious
tone enlivens an otherwise quite vacuous poem, "The Red-

[6] *The Poetical Works,* p. 83.

breast Chasing the Butterfly." In the first stanza, for example, the poet gives a long string of national names for the "pious Bird" whom man loves best: Peter in Norway, Thomas in Finland and Russia, Hans in Germany, and Frederick in France.

> The Bird whom by some name or other
> All men who know thee call their Brother,
> The darling of Children and Men! [11–13]

This list, then, much longer in manuscript than in published form, is undercut by these anticlimactic lines: "Could Father Adam open his eyes" (Father Adam, we should recall, named the birds and beasts upon opening his eyes)

> And see this sight beneath the skies,
> He'd wish to close them again. [15–16]

Later the poet confronts the wayward bird with the pious and commonplace tale, preserved in ballads and elsewhere, of the robins that covered the bodies of the children lost in the forest. The glaring incongruity between the children's fate and the butterfly's danger is offered in the same half-serious, half-playful tone. For the poet then proceeds to invoke the sacred ideal of brotherhood:

> His beautiful wings in crimson are dress'd,
> As if he were bone of thy bone. [39–40]

And later in 1807 the line becomes, "A brother he seems of thy own." But the poem ends, curiously, with a vague threat,

> If thou would be happy in thy nest,
> O pious Bird whom man loves best
> Love him, or leave him alone! [41–43]

These lines might be construed as a humorous anticlimax. The lameness of the alternative, to leave the butterfly alone, mocks man's futile attempt to impose a moral, or even a humane, code upon the creatures of nature. But in its fuzziness it may also suggest retaliation, and the poem, because of its lack of definiteness, does not succeed. In "Foresight" Wordsworth does offer, at least in the 1802 version, a unified comic conception of the overbearing elder brother:

> Do not touch it; summers two
> I am older, Anne, than you.[7]

And in "The Sun has long been set" a broader city-country antithesis is established, largely through recollecting the lines by Burns in the second part; [8] but the effect is mildly, if somewhat complacently, satirical:

> Who would go parading
> In London, and masquerading,
> On such a night of June
> With that beautiful soft half moon;
> And all these innocent blisses
> On such a night as this is! [10–15]

Two poems advance beyond these inept forays into satire. Ford Swetnam has shown, in his study of the evolution of the many satiric voices adopted by Wordsworth throughout his career, that "The Barberry Tree" is a debate, similar to

[7] Lines 7–8. There are at least two good reasons for not reading these last two poems as mildly satiric in tone. Wordsworth added a pompous footnote, on De Quincey's suggestion, to the passage quoted from "The Redbreast and the Butterfly" in 1815: "See *Paradise Lost,* Book XI, where Adam points out to Eve the ominous sign of the Eagle chasing 'two Birds of gayest plume,' and the gentle Hart and Hind pursued by their enemy." Also in 1815 he added to "Foresight" eight lines in the voice of a moralizing adult. It is possible, however, that what was once amusing no longer seemed so (*PW,* 2:149; 1:228, ll. 25–32).

[8] "The Twa Dogs," lines 124–125; identified by Thomas Hutchinson, *Poems in Two Volumes,* 2:187.

"Expostulation and Reply," in which the poet as innocent fool takes on the critics who ridicule his poetry. The strength and beauty of his vision of the natural scene, the leafy morris dance of the barberry tree, win the argument by simple demonstration. And "These chairs," Swetnam argues, is Wordsworth's reply to Coleridge's "Dejection: An Ode," "a parody of the philosophical position" of his frend's poem, "coupled with a reaffirmation of the philosophy of the one life." [9]

The great metrical freedom of these last two poems leads us to one final consideration. Wordsworth began experimenting with the sonnet early in 1802, after ten years had lapsed since his last efforts in that form. During the summer and fall of 1802 a flood of sonnets poured from him and he continued to write them throughout his lifetime, over five hundred in all.[10] He elected the sonnet (having "taken fire" from his reading of Milton's sonnets) [11] as a form peculiarly suited to his needs:

> In truth the prison, unto which we doom
> Ourselves, no prison is: and hence for me,
> In sundry moods, 'twas pastime to be bound
> Within the Sonnet's scanty plot of ground;
> Pleased if some Souls (for such there needs must be)

[9] Ford Swetnam, "Wordsworth's Satiric Voice" (Cornell University Ph.D. dissertation, 1967), *DA*, xxviii, 2265-A, pp. 69, 79.

[10] Fifty-six sonnets appeared in *Poems* (1807); all but one were composed between January 1802 and January 1807. See Hutchinson's "Note on the Wordsworthian Sonnet," *Poems in Two Volumes* (1897), 1:208–226, and his notes to individual sonnets.

[11] *DWJ*, 164, 21 May (1802); in the Fenwick note Wordsworth identifies the sonnet "I grieved for Bounaparte" as one of three he wrote in 1801 [1802] after hearing Milton's sonnets (*Prose Works*, ed. Alexander B. Grosart [London, 1876], 3:52, 53).

Who have felt the weight of too much liberty,
Should find brief solace there, as I have found.[12]

Yet during that spring Wordsworth was imposing a variety of "bounds" upon his poetry. Thomas Hutchinson has marked the progress "in the variety of rhythms essayed by him in these two volumes [1807], and in the high proportion of his successes over his failures." The special quality of these rhythms was first noticed by Walter Pater, in 1874. He wrote, in an essay on Wordsworth, that "some of his pieces, pieces prompted by a sort of half-playful mysticism, . . . are noticeable for a certain quaint gaiety of metre, and rival by their perfect execution in this respect similar pieces among our own Elizabethan . . . poetry." [13] Thomas Hutchinson attributes the poet's "advance in metrical facility" primarily to his study of Chaucer and the Elizabethans, after his arrival at Grasmere. He gives particularly high praise to the octosyllabic measure, a couplet, he claims, taught to the poet by Jonson and others, especially Milton in "L'Allegro" and "Il Penseroso"; he also points out the metrical debt that the three Daisy poems owe to Jonson's "Song i" of "Eupheme" in *Underwoods* and to Drayton's "Nymphidia." Miss Darbishire has extended this knowledge with a chart of the various metrical forms and their probable sources, most of which, it turns out, are traceable to sixteenth- and seventeenth-century poems.[14] But apart from direct borrowing— not really very extensive, one must admit—a number of effects seem to derive from Wordsworth's adaptation of

[12] *PW*, 3:1, 2, lines 8–14.
[13] "On Wordsworth," *Fortnightly Review* 88 N.S. (1874): 463.
[14] Hutchinson's remarks are in his Introduction to *Poems in Two Volumes* (1897), 1:x–xii, n. 1. Miss Darbishire's chart is in Appendix II of her *Wordsworth, Poems in Two Volumes*, pp. 464–470; see also her introduction, p. xxxix.

certain techniques common among Elizabethan and Jacobean poets.

Wordsworth's theoretical interest in meter goes back to the very beginning of his poetic career. In the 1800 Preface, and especially in the revisions and additions of 1802, he gives meter, as Stephen Parrish has shown, "unique prominence, as the single discriminant of verse." [15] "Meter," Wordsworth wrote in the long addition to the Preface, "obeys certain laws" that do not interfere with "passion" except "to heighten and improve the pleasure which co-exists with it." Pleasure, in its turn, is both "the grand elementary principle" of art and its "immediate" goal.[16] The recurrence of the semi-technical term "pleasure" [17] in Wordsworth's own comments during the period of composition and preparation for the press of the lyrics of 1802 attests to his great interest in metrical experiments and suggests the importance of their effect on these poems.

Before 1802 he had given the traditional ballad stanza and its many variations about as many turns as it was capable of. In it he had achieved the harsh bluntness of "Goody Blake and Harry Gill," the rollicking high spirits of "Exposulation and Reply," and the surprisingly delicate effects of the Lucy poems. If the metrical experiments in 1802 cohere at all in this sudden swing to variety of form, it is in their common

[15] Stephen M. Parrish, "Wordsworth and Coleridge on Meter" *JEGP*, 59 (1960): 43.

[16] 1802, *LCW*, 55, 51, 50. See Parrish, "Wordsworth and Coleridge on Meter," pp. 45–49.

[17] Cf. "profitable pleasure" quoted above, Chapter 1. See Parrish, "Wordsworth and Coleridge on Meter," on the term "pleasure": "At once a psychological, aesthetic, almost an epistemological term, pleasure was the 'grand elementary principle' of man's nature, the distinctive achievement of poetic art, and something like an instrument of truth" (p. 46).

element of lightness and joyousness, their common effects. Often their "tripping" quality contributes to the comic or near comic effects already mentioned. "The Redbreast Chasing the Butterfly," "Foresight," and especially "The cock is crowing" have the breathless movement one associates with children's verse or, perhaps, with the musical effusions of the early sixteenth-century "courtly makers," for example in the untitled poem,

> Pleasure it is
> To hear, I wis,
> The birds sing;
> The deer in the dale,
> The sheep in the vale,
> The corn springing [18]

or with the sophisticated poems by Robert Herrick like "To Cherry-blossomes" or "To the Lark." [19] In "The Sun has long been set" and "To a Skylark" the satiric descent that occurs at the end of each poem is marked by a faltering, hesitant rhythm:

> Who would go parading
> In London, and masquerading. [10–11]

[18] Attributed to William Cornish (d. 1524?), *Poetry of the English Renaissance* (New York, 1957), ed. J. William Hebel and Hoyt H. Hudson, p. 42. Wordsworth admired Skelton's verse (*LY*, 2:638, 7 January 1833, W. W. to Alexander Dyce). Cf. Skelton's "To Mistress Isabel Pennell,"

> My maiden Isabel
> Reflaring rosabel
> The flagrant camamell,
>   The ruddy rosary,
>   The sovereign rosemary,
>   The pretty strawberry,
>   The columbine, the nepte, etc. [4–10]

[19] *The Poetical Works*, pp. 74, 87.

I on earth will go plodding on
By myself, chearfully till the day is done. [30–31]

And in "Among all lovely things" the easy-going, tauto-
logical narrative is further loosened by frequent enjambment, an effect modulated in the heavily pointed *Poems*
(1807).

Wordsworth might well have learned to work enjambment against a tightly organized meter from the more accomplished Elizabethans and Jacobeans. Ben Jonson, for example, in "Why I write not of Love" and "To Penshurst,"
both poems much admired by Wordsworth, employs run-on
lines for contrast and emphasis.[20] In several of Wordsworth's poems enjambment occurs apparently at random
(the two poems "To the Daisy") or because of an unfamiliar
or awkwardly handled meter (both poems "To the Celandine"). But in the best poems the poet is in control. In the
second Butterfly poem enjambment occurs in two places
only, within the otherwise severely end-stopped stanzas. The
line spills over in pointed contrast to the fixed image it
bears: "not frozen seas / More motionless" (5–6). At the end
of the poem, the lengthened days of childhood memory, are
reproduced by the enjambment:

[20] *DWJ*, 116, 129 (11 February and 9 March 1802). Cf. from the first
Jonson poem, an example of contrast:

It is enough, they once did get
Mars and my Mother, in their net.   [*Poems,* p. 93, ll. 6–7]

and from the second, an example of emphasis:

Thou art not, *Penshurst*, built to envious show,
Of touch, or marble; nor canst boast a row
Of polish'd pillars, or a roof of gold. [*Poems,* p. 93, ll. 1–3]

Both poems are in *British Poets*, 4:552.

> Sweet childish days that were as long
> As twenty days are now. [18–19]

The most striking image in "The Green Linnet" is further emphasized by the run-on lines:

> the flutter of his wings
> Upon his back and body flings
> Shadows and sunny glimmerings. [29–31]

More impressive, perhaps, are the effects achieved in four of the "recovery" poems. In the first stanza of "The Sparrow's Nest," in which the startled memory leaps from present to past, the lines spill over with surprising frequency. In the first Butterfly poem the pattern is reversed for a different effect. Stanza one is without metrical variation: the still butterfly is "caught" in the closed pattern of verse. But the movement and exuberance of stanza two are supported by the many run-on lines. The nine occurrences of run-ons in the thirty-two lines of "To a Cuckoo" also reflect mental and physical movement within the poem. And finally, "My heart leaps up" begins and ends its exposition of the theme of continuity by appearing to lengthen lines one and two through enjambment, and by extending *and* running-on the last two lines.

Wordsworth, often in contrast to his sixteenth- and seventeenth-century models, took liberties with metrical form when he felt it appropriate. The high frequency of sight-rhymes, near-rhymes, and feminine rhymes, particularly in the Skylark and flower poems, corresponds to the relative levity of these poems, while the firmer lines and more precise rhymes complement the more serious lyrics like "To a Cuckoo," the first Butterfly poem, and "The Sparrow's Nest." The former poems appear to sacrifice wit and elegance for a looser, more wayward and personal form, ideally suited for the "moods of mind" he wished to reveal.

Besides the many different stanzaic patterns, Wordsworth was experimenting with different ode forms as well throughout the spring of 1802. He had regarded the Tintern Abbey "Lines" as essentially odic in manner and tone. He had not "ventured to call this Poem an Ode; but it was written with a hope that in the transitions, and the impassioned movement of the versification, would be found the principal requisites of that species of composition." [21] The Tintern Abbey poem is, nevertheless, in blank verse. However, the open lyric form (retaining meter and rhyme) with which Wordsworth began working early in 1802 reveals itself in various stages of development among the poems of that period.

In "The Redbreast Chasing the Butterfly" the verse seems to move at random, in unsatisfactory imitation, perhaps, of the movements of the two creatures about the garden. In later revisions Wordsworth added and subtracted lines with great frequency, apparently never quite happy with the poem's effect. In "To a Skylark" again the verse moves rapidly, but it is nervous, almost hysterical in tone, achieving something like the effect of a recording played at too high a speed. The transitions are abrupt indeed and the final one, perhaps by intention, deflates the ebullient spirits so eagerly sought after in the first part. The movement of "These chairs they have no words to utter" is appropriately slower, if somewhat stilted. But the use of internal rhymes, usually of long open sounds ("no . . . stone . . . alone . . . sorrow," "without . . . thou . . . now") and the momentary change of pace in stanza three (14–20) give the

21 *PW*, 2:517, from Wordsworth's note to the 1800 edition.

poem some flexibility and grace, and together with the repetitions ("Dead, dead / Dead" and "Peace, peace, peace"), an-appropriate somberness.

Showing considerable lyric promise and control, as well as happy rhythmic effects, is the strange "new" poem, "The Barberry Tree." Its deliberately awkward self-parody and satiric tautology are set off against brilliant effects of rhythm and sound:

> And mingling breath and murmur'd motion
> Like eddies of the gusty ocean,
> Do in their leafy morris bear
> Mirth and gladness thro the air:
> As up and down the branches toss,
> And above and beneath and across
> The breezes brush on lusty pinion
> Sportive struggling for dominion. [29–36]

Or the more musically varied passage just before the end:

> The piping leaves will not be heard.
>   But when the wind rushes
>   Thro brakes and thro bushes;
> And around, and within, and without,
>   Makes a roar and a rout;
>   Then may you see
>   The Barberry-tree;
>   With all its yellow flow'rs
>   And interwoven bow'rs:
>   Toss in merry madness
>   Ev'ry bough of gladness:
> And dance to and fro to the loud-singing breeze,
> The blithest of gales, and the maddest of trees. [94–106]

Here internal rhymes and sound patterns, as well as the somewhat familiar end-rhymes, in conjunction with the fluent lines of verse, help to render most effectively the joyous moment being stored up by the poet in defiance of his cavilling critics. One cannot help but think, too, that Wordsworth's experiments in these poems provide the technique for the more formal but no less supple patterns of "My heart leaps up" and the great "Immortality Ode," where efforts only partly successful before now coalesce in rich and deep-voiced music:

> The Rainbow comes and goes
> And lovely is the rose
> The moon doth with delight
> Look round her when the heavens are bare
> Waters on a starry night
> Are beautiful and fair
> The sunshine is a glorious birth
> But yet I know where'er I go
> That there hath pass'd away a glory from the earth.
>
> [10–18]

Critics have suggested before that Wordsworth was influenced by Jonson's odes in the composition of his own "Ode." [22] That winter and spring, when reading Jonson's verse and disputing with Coleridge over it,[23] he was no doubt impressed with Jonson's happy union of freedom and control. For he learned to sing from the older poets; perhaps he gained some of their grace, their understated rhythms, and what Pater has called their "quaint gaiety of meter." He caught little of their sharpness of wit and high

---

[22] J. D. Rea, "Coleridge's Intimations of Immortality from Proclus," *Modern Philology* 26 (1928): 203–204; Herbert Hartman, "The 'Intimations' of Wordsworth's 'Ode'," *RES* 6 (1930): 136–138. They cite the "Ode to the Immortal Memory and Friendship of that Noble Fair Sir Lucius Cary and Sir H. Morison," lines 65–74; Wordsworth would not have been impressed by the "metaphysical" opening stanzas.

[23] *DWJ*, 137, 19 March 1802.

sense of form, however, and only rarely their amused detachment. In the short poem, Wordsworth has taken up their quite "social" song-form and made it into something personal, almost private, conveying, again in the words of Pater, "a sort of half-playful mysticism."

BIBLIOGRAPHICAL NOTE

Some help on Wordsworth's versification in these poems can be found in Thomas Hutchinson's edition of *Poems in Two Volumes* (Oxford, 1897), 1:xi–xii, and in Helen Darbishire's notes and Appendix II of her edition of the same book. Of theoretical interest is Stephen M. Parrish's "Wordsworth and Coleridge on Meter," *JEGP* 59 (1960): 41–49.

[6]

Toward the Language of Vision: Two Versions of "Resolution and Independence"

First called "The Leech-Gatherer" when it was begun in the spring of 1802, Wordsworth's "Resolution and Independence" has long been troublesome to critics. Coleridge was the first to remark on its "disharmony in style," finding it "characteristic of the author" in its blend of "defect" and "excellence." Since then critics have attempted to explain or illustrate, reharmonize or play down the "inconstancy" of style in the poem, the abrupt shifts from sublimity to "matter-of-factness" that so exercised Coleridge.[1] Perhaps if we look closely at the evolution of "Resolution and Independence," we can learn how the two apparently warring elements, sublimity and matter-of-factness, came to be present in the poem, and can even discover their ultimate harmony.

Coleridge linked Wordsworth's excessive attention to "fact" with the literal focus of lyrical ballads like "The Thorn." No one would seriously argue that "The Leech-Gatherer" belongs among the lyrical ballads. For one thing the poet has chosen an 'artful' Spenserian stanza which gives his poem a very un-ballad-like sound and progression. The persona, too, has moved to center stage, no longer

[1] *BL*, 2:95, 96, 100, 101.

97

merely relating and commenting on the doings and undoing of the figures he observes. Moreover, the poem is removed by a period of at least four years from the composition of any of the central lyrical ballads published together under that title in 1798. However, an analysis of the poet's revisions will show, I believe, how deeply the poem was rooted in the mode of the lyrical ballad and how crucial a stage it was in the formation of a further range of voice. The poet's breakthrough from the language of men to the language of vision takes place in the process of his composing and revising this important poem.

Dorothy Wordsworth's description of the event on which the poem was based reveals the major component of the early version. In 1800 she writes in her journal, with characteristic precision, that she and her brother encountered an old man, while walking, who was bent "almost double."

He had on a coat, thrown over his shoulders, above his waistcoat and coat. Under this he carried a bundle, and had an apron on and a night-cap. His face was interesting. He had dark eyes and a long nose. . . . He was of Scotch parents, but had been born in the army. He had had a wife, and 'a good woman, and it pleased God to bless us with ten children'. All these were dead but one, of whom he had not heard for many years, a sailor. His trade was to gather leeches, but now leeches are scarce, and he had not strength for it. He lived by begging, and was making his way to Carlisle, where he should buy a few godly books to sell. He said leeches were very scarce, partly owing to this dry season, but many years they have been scarce—he supposed it owing to their being much sought after, that they did not breed fast, and were of slow growth. . . . He had been hurt in driving a cart, his leg broke, his body driven over, his skull fractured. He felt no pain till he recovered from his first insensibility.[2]

2 *DWJ*, 56–57.

98

In 1952 Helen Darbishire published the variants from a notebook kept by Sara Hutchinson in which she copied poems by Wordsworth and Coleridge during and after the period Wordsworth was working on "Resolution and Independence." In Miss Darbishire's succinct account we learn:

> He cut out the stanza ["He seem'd like one who little saw or heard," see LG:57–63] . . . and put in its place that stanza which is surely the imaginative core of the poem ["As a huge stone, etc.," RI:64–70]. . . . Further he cut out from the Leech-gatherer's speech his account of his family's losses, and some at least of his difficulties over the leeches.[3]

When it has served their argument critics have made use of the last of Miss Darbishire's discoveries, noting with considerable relief how Wordsworth had the good sense to omit "the details of the old man's history." [4] No one, however, has pursued her supposition about additions to the poem.

A comparison of the two earliest manuscript versions, stanza by stanza and line by line, reveals not a mere deletion or two and a single, if remarkable addition, but very nearly two distinct poems, different in conception, execution and effect.[5] The first version, which for clarity's sake will be

[3] *PW*, 2:536.

[4] Hyman, p. 118; Gérard, p. 129; see John Jones, *The Egotistical Sublime* (London, 1954, 1960), 62; Moorman, 1:543. Conran seems confused when he talks of Wordsworth's "first imaginative intuition of the old man" as the rock-sea-beast figure (p. 66; see below, p. 113).

[5] A. W. Thomson, in his essay on the poem, considers the revisions in summary fashion and concludes, as I do, that the second version "is essentially a different poem." His emphasis is on the greater psychological subtlety of the second poem, "its complex interplay between self-communing and communication" (*Wordsworth's Mind and Art,* ed. A. W. Thomson [Edinburgh, 1969], p. 194). William Heath, in *Wordsworth and Coleridge* (1970), presents a somewhat different picture of the relationship between the two poems, missing, I think,

called "The Leech-Gatherer" (*LG*), was begun on May 3, 1802, "finished" on May 7, and regarded as quite unalterable on June 14 when William and Dorothy wrote a letter of instruction and reproof to Sara and Mary Hutchinson in response to their criticism of Wordsworth's poem. The poem was no doubt read to Coleridge on May 4, but no record of his opinion of the first version survives, except as it may have influenced the Hutchinson sisters' objections. In any case the consequence of their advice was that on July 2 Dorothy transcribed "the alterations" in "The Leech-Gatherer" and on July 5 it was sent to Coleridge as a "finished" poem. This poem is substantially the one published in 1807 as "Resolution and Independence" (RI).[6]

In the letter to the Hutchinson sisters Wordsworth defends his diction as coincident with "the language of men." To Mary he urges the rightness of expressions like "viewing" the old man "for a length of time" and "sickness had by him." The first phrase is right, he argues, because it suggests duration as the verb "seeing" would not. And the second is justified because it is a "phrase which anybody might use." He then attempts to persuade Sara that "the latter part of the Leech-gatherer," which had displeased her, is of a piece with the first part. Again he defends its plainness, its deliberate flatness. Against the expectation of "almost something spiritual or supernatural" he brings forward " 'a lonely place, a Pond' 'by which an old man *was*, far from all house or home'—not stood, not sat but '*was*'—the figure presented in the most naked simplicity possible."

---

their distinctness from one another (pp. 120–139). My own essay, written before either of these was published, studies the relationships between the two poems in detail. See the parallel texts and the description of manuscripts which follow.

[6] *DWJ*, 155, 158, 159, 172, 186; *EY*, 1:364–367; see Moorman, 1:544.

Seeking to explain this presence to himself and to his reader, Wordsworth says, "I then describe him." There is no figure available to his imagination, he goes on, "more impressive than that of an old Man like this, the survivor of a Wife and ten children, travelling alone among the mountains and all lonely places, carrying with him his own fortitude, and the necessities which an unjust state of society has entailed upon him." [7]

Now if we look at the manuscript of "The Leech-Gatherer," we shall find this emphasis borne out in considerable detail. The particularity that Wordsworth clings to in his defense of the poem is found as early as lines 57 and following:

> He seem'd like one who little saw or heard
> For chimney-nook, or bed, or coffin meet
> A stick was in his hand wherewith he stirr'd
> The waters of the pond beneath his feet. [LG:57–60]

The next two stanzas further augment the physical description, but the first (LG:64–70), picturing his bent frame, was retained in the published version (1807) and the second (LG:71–77), having to do with the old man's cloak and bundle, remained in manuscript versions until proof was made for the 1807 edition. The passage, referred to in the letter, that gives the man's life history and catalogue of troubles must have included both the twenty-six lines torn from the manuscript (99–124), and the lines that follow (127–133). The word "home" appearing at line 106 is not much to go on, but it does not contradict the biography Wordsworth summarizes in his letter ("survivor of a Wife and ten children, travelling alone"). The lines that survive form the climax of the first version:

[7] EY, 1:366.

I yet can gain my bread tho' in times gone
I twenty could have found where now I can find one

Feeble I am in health these hills to climb
Yet I procure a Living of my own
This is my summer work in winter time
I go with godly Books from Town to Town
Now I am seeking Leeches up & down
From house to house I go from Barn to Barn
All over Cartmell Fells & up to Blellan Tarn.

[LG:125–133]

In the old man's speech ("the language of men" as spoken
by "grave livers") Wordsworth hoped to arouse the reader's
interest, not bore him. But he also seemed certain that the
voice itself would achieve the miracle, would turn the reader
around, as the poet was turned, to face himself. He reasons
thus in the letter to the Hutchinsons, "It is in the character
of the old man to tell his story in a manner which an im-
patient reader must necessarily feel as tedious. But Good
God! Such a figure, in such a place, a pious self-respecting,
miserably infirm . . . Old Man telling such a tale!" The
emphasis falls not upon the poet's imaginative response to
the old man, but squarely upon the character telling his own
tale. For when the tale is complete, the poem is over. The
concluding stanza follows:

With this the Old Man other matter blended
Which he deliver'd with demeanor kind
Yet stately in the main & when he ended
I could have laugh'd myself to scorn to find
In that decrepit man so firm a mind
God said I be my help & stay secure
I'll think of the Leech-gatherer on the lonely Moor.

At this point in the development of the poem Wordsworth
did not perceive the poem's uniqueness. The remarkable

opening section is more like a self-reflexive lyric than a ballad with its meditative central figure, the poet himself, or, as Anthony Conran and Geoffrey Hartman have suggested, the dreamer-poet in an allegorical dream-vision.[8] Yet Wordsworth linked the poem with "The Thorn" and "The Idiot Boy." He evidently saw it, as he tells Sara in his letter, as a study in "the old man's character." Dorothy describes it more frankly as a poem written "to illustrate a particular character or truth." [9] In other words, though he has rooted the poem in what is personal and "lyrical," he still conceives of it, in substance, as a "ballad" that describes another's character.

Only two months earlier he had begun writing again after nearly two years of silence. The first poems in a series of more than thirty poems written in the spring of 1802 were three lyrical ballads in the old manner, "The Sailor's Mother," "Alice Fell," and "Beggars." All three poems depict an encounter between the poet-traveller and a beggar, a wandering and alien figure who gives the poet pause. As such they offer an instructive parallel to "The Leech-Gatherer." In the first, a woman traveller, "not old though something past her prime," strikes him as "Majestic . . . as a mountain storm," and reminds him of the noble past, or a "Roman Matron," expressing in the present moment an "ancient spirit" not yet dead (3–7). She inspires in him a pride in the country that has "bred / Such strength, a dignity so fair" (9–10). As in "The Leech-Gatherer" the poet asks a leading question, for her burden, like the old man's "bulky Pack" (LG:75), arouses his curiosity (15–18). Her answer, filling the nineteen remaining lines of the poem, tells her "simple" but heavy story, the loss of her eldest son at sea, the "weary way" (29) she has travelled to see to his

---

[8] Conran, pp. 66ff.; Hartman, pp. 266–273.   [9] *EY*, 1:367.

belongings, including the incongruous and pathetic memento, the singing bird:

> ". . . and neat and trim
> "He kept it—many voyages
> "This singing-bird hath gone with him;
> "And I, God help me! for my little wit
> "Trail't with me, Sir! he took so much delight in it!"
>
> [32–36]

Here the poet has not provided his own response, but in the manner of "The Forsaken Indian Maiden" or "The Female Vagrant" he has let the speaker's voice do its own work. As he says of the latter, "The Woman thus her artless story told."

In "Alice Fell" the situation is altered to present the dramatic crisis as retold by the poet after the event; and since the wandering spirit is a child, attached only to "Durham," which seems indifferent to her, and to her ruined cloak, she must be questioned closely to elicit her "story." But the effect is curiously similar to that achieved elsewhere by elderly garrulousness. The child's speech, sparse as it is, and her expressive tears, are in a way the joint language of the poem's "imaginative core":

> "Whither are you going, Child?
> Tonight along these lonesome ways?"
> "To Durham" answer'd she half wild. [33–35]

> "My Child in Durham do you dwell?"
> She check'd herself in her distress
> And said "my name is Alice Fell,
> I'm fatherless and motherless.
>
> And I to Durham, Sir, belong." [41–45]

The new cloak, provided generously but somewhat pomp-
ously by the narrator on the next day, seems anticlimactic,
the child's pride slightly tainted (53–60).

The third poem, "Beggars," combines the garrulous adult
and the almost silent but entirely expressive child in one
poem. The beggar woman first encountered by the poet is of
a stature reminiscent of the Sailor's Mother ("a tall man's
height or more," line 1) but suggests more exotic places and
more distant times:

> Her face was of Egyptian brown;
> Fit person was she for a queen
> To head those ancient Amazonian files
> Or ruling Banditt's wife among the Grecian Isles.   [9–12]

Wordsworth does not render her speech, however—an interesting decision in light of his final treatment of the Leech-
gatherer's speech. Instead she begs from him, "Pouring out
sorrow like a sea / Grief after grief" (14–15). Dubious of her
truthfulness the poet rewards her beauty:

> —"And yet some small assistance you shall have
> And for your beauty's sake—you are a woman brave."
> [17–18]

In the "second part" of the poem he describes his encounter
with two "Boys at play," plainly the children of the woman
he had just given alms to. Their speech is not to be trusted
either, for they beg for coins by claiming to be orphans.
Their real speech is their actions, their gaiety, the pleasure
they take in each other, in their natural surroundings (the
butterfly and flowers), and in the "game" of begging. The
chief features common to all three poems are the alien
quality of the wanderers, their surprising self-sufficiency even
as beggars or waifs, and the important role speech plays in
their dramatization and final effectiveness as character

sketches. Not surprisingly the early "Leech-Gatherer" shares the same features and is remarkable only in its striking and beautiful opening stanzas. In the light of this discussion, we can assume that Wordsworth regarded "The Leech-Gatherer," as he did "The Sailor's Mother," "Alice Fell," and "Beggars," as another variation on the lyrical ballad.[10]

If we look now at the cuts and substitutions made in the interval between the letter of June 14 and the version of July 5, Wordsworth's changing conception of the poem will become clear. In place of the domestic simile, hardly a simile, describing what the man "seem'd like" (LG:57–60), Wordsworth gives first a literal, "naked" description of a "motionless" figure at the side of the pond (RI:57–63), followed by the brilliant double simile that slides easily from the starkly natural realm onto the edge of a terrifying fantasy:

> As a huge stone is sometimes seen to lie
> Couch'd on the bald top of an eminence,
> Wonder to all that do the same espy,
> By what means it could thither come & whence;
> So that it seems a thing endued with sense,
> Like a Sea-beast crawl'd forth, which on a shelf
> Of rock or sand reposeth, there to sun itself.[11]

[10] They were begun early enough—March 11, 1802—for Wordsworth to have considered them for inclusion in the 1802 edition of *Lyrical Ballads*, for which he had been preparing additions to the Preface.

[11] RI:64–70. W. W. Robson has suggested that Wordsworth's later removal, in 1815, of the previous lines,

> My course I stopp'd as soon as I espied
> The Old Man in the naked wilderness;
> Close by a Pond upon the hither side
> He stood alone: a minute's space, I guess,
> I watch'd him, he continuing motionless.

After the lines on the man's doubled frame Wordsworth adds another simile which, like its more daring predecessor, urges the merely human into the two realms of nature and fantasy:

> Motionless as a cloud the Old Man stood,
> That heareth not the loud winds when they call,
> And moveth altogether if it moves at all.   [RI:82-84]

As metaphors, however, these figures do not function to clothe the thought, but rather, as Wordsworth says in the Preface to *Poems* (1815), to "divest" and "strip" the man of ordinary prosaic life, leaving him in isolated, elemental and mysterious simplicity.[12] If words are not "an incarnation of the thought," Wordsworth wrote in the third "Essay upon Epitaphs" (1810), "but only a clothing for it, then surely they will prove an ill gift."[13]

It is impossible to tell from the manuscript in what order Wordsworth made the changes that follow. In linear sequence they are: first, the excision of five stanzas of the old man's speech (LG:99-133); second, the substitution of a brief summary of what he said,

> He told me that he to the Pond had come
> To gather Leeches, being old and poor,

> To the Pool's further margin then I drew,
> He all the while before me being full in view   [RI:59-63]

served to sharpen the contrast between the poet as the egotistical center of interest and the animate-inanimate, but non-human, figure of the old man (Robson, p. 128). In fact this process had begun earlier with the addition of the visionary lines, and continued in time as he changed "espied" to "saw" (1804) and "lonely place" to "a Pool bare to the eye of Heaven" (1820) in the previous stanza (RI:52). The later changes however are apt adjustments.

[12] *PW*, 2:438; see Robson, p. 129.   [13] *LCW*, 125.

> That 'twas his calling, better far than some
> Though he had many hardships to endure:
> From Pond to Pond he roam'd from Moor to Moor,
> Housing with God's good help by choice or chance,
> And in this way he gain'd an honest maintenance.
>
> [RI:113–119]

and third, the introduction of a third simile, a double one, which carries forward the work of the first two:

> The Old Man still stood talking by my side,
> But soon his voice to me was like a stream
> Scarce heard, nor word from word could I divide,
> And the whole body of the Man did seem
> Like one [wh]om I had met with in a dream;
> Or like a Man from some far region sent
> To give me human strength, & strong admonishment.
>
> [RI:120–126]

One obvious effect of these similes is to present figures of the imagination which do the task that Wordsworth thought had been accomplished by his quoting the old man's speech; they are images of the poet's turning mind which serve thus to turn the reader's mind. While at first the poet had placed the source of power in the affecting narrative, he now finds that power in the "coalescing" and "shaping" action of his own language.[14] This action *is* the turning of his own mind at the time of composition, and turns the reader's mind, as a spoken tale could not, by demanding recognition as an emblem of experience rather than as experience itself. As emblems, then, all three passages function to pull the old man out of his literalness into the realm of myth, onto a level of consciousness above or below the moral "pleasure" derived merely from "contemplating" what Wordsworth

[14] *LCW* (1815 Preface), 149.

called in his letter "the fortitude, independence, persevering spirit, and the general moral dignity of this old man's character."

Given these changes, it is now possible for Wordsworth to unite the "latter part" of the poem with the opening stanzas. He adds this stanza which harks back to his initial depression in the midst of Nature's glorious process:

> My former thoughts return'd, the fear that kills,
> The hope that is unwilling to be fed,
> Cold, pain, and labour, & all fleshly ills,
> And mighty Poets in their misery dead;
> And now, not knowing what the Old Man had said,
> My question eagerly did I renew,
> "How is it that you live? & what is it you do?"
>
> [RI:127–133]

The repeated question brings a repeated but still summarized response:

> He with a smile did then his words repeat
> And said, that wheresoe'er they might be spied
> He gather'd Leeches, stirring at his feet
> The waters in the Ponds where they abide.
>
> [RI:134–137]

As before, all trace of the old man's peculiar speech has been removed. In the first version he himself had said:

> I yet can gain my bread tho' in times gone
> I twenty could have found where now I can find one.
>
> [LG:125–126]

Then he had proceeded to give an account of his means of "procuring" a "Living" (LG:127–133) winter and summer. In the second version Wordsworth unifies the old man's occupations and reduces his garrulousness to a three-line précis:

Once he could meet with them on every side;
But fewer they became from day to day,
And so his means of life before him died away.
[RI:138–140]

Finally, not with a simile, or even double simile, but with a frankly mythical vision, Wordsworth writes in these lines:

While he was talking thus the lonely place,
The Old Man's shape & speech all troubl'd me;
In my mind's eye I seem'd to see him pace
About the weary Moors continually,
Wandering about alone and silently. [RI:141–145]

The choice of verbs is important: in the mind's eye the poet sees him both *pace* (with a sense of purpose) and *wander* (without ceasing, without ever reaching his destination). The old man at this point shares with Tantalus and Sisyphus, with the Wandering Jew and the old man of Chaucer's "Pardoner's Tale," just this quality of purposive but ceaseless activity, a quality that seems, on the authority of my examples, at least, the essence of myth. Thus fabled by the imagination, "the mind's eye," Wordsworth's old man is lifted out of the immediate circumstances as he was in the previous stanza, but now retains his own shape, becomes his own metaphor.

Critics have read the final version of the poem from three different angles. They see the poet as having shifted back from the nightmare world of metaphor and myth to the solid world of good sense, or as having moved forward from the world of fact to the world of vision, or as having arrived at some middle ground, by achieving a reconciliation between the two worlds, or by resting in comforting or in disquieting simultaneity.[15] If we are to learn from the poet's

15 Nightmare to good sense, Conran, pp. 66, 77; fact to vision, Harold Bloom, *The Visionary Company: A Reading of English Romantic*

revisions, however, we must emphasize the interior nature of the tale finally told. What Wordsworth discovered in writing this poem, as he worked his way from the ballad-like beginnings to the fable-like effect of the last version, was the special power of figurative language not only to delight the mind but also to transform it, to give it a range and depth it did not have before the man became metaphor. This discovery will not allow us to see reconcilation or simultaneity as the poem's final effect, nor find, with any certainty, the journey toward or away from myth to be its essential point. The poem's greatness lies in its complex rendering of inner turmoil, in its developed series of figures leading to a pure Wordsworthian counter-image, and in its persuasive fusion of the old and the new voices.

In this light we can now consider the poem's "moral" conclusion. The spoken peripety remains the same in both versions. Originally a tribute to the old man's "moral dignity," in its new context it becomes a sign of the great inner distance travelled by the poet. No longer merely an earnest statement of the lesson learned, it impresses one as an utterance made in sudden relief from the intense experience just undergone.

> "God," said I, "be my help & stay secure!
> "I'll think of the Leech-gatherer on the lonely Moor.["]

By thus tempering the language of men, Wordsworth was able to shape the language of vision: a language which enabled him to transform a poem divided and confused in purpose and effect into one that still contains both voices but in meaningful relationship and final unity.

Poetry (London, 1961), pp. 164, 165; reconciliation, Gérard, pp. 130, 131; simultaneity that is comforting, Grob, "Process and Permanence in 'Resolution and Independence,' " *ELH* 18 (1961): 90, 97–100; or disquieting, Hartman, pp. 268–270.

For we look in vain for this new language in the whole range of lyrical ballads from the darker tales of 1797–1798, "The Thorn" and "Goody Blake and Harry Gill," to the mellower pieces composed in 1802 that have been discussed above. The signs of the new voice are apparent, however, in the "Immorality Ode," begun in 1802, and the group of poems, short lyrics and blank verse pieces, composed in that same spring. Among these perhaps the best known are "To the Cuckoo," the two "Butterfly" poems, and "A Farewell." In "Resolution and Independence" the new voice emerges in response to the old voice in a manner unique to that poem. It is as though, as Wallace Stevens has written, the poem were an "insatiable actor" that "slowly and / With meditation" speaks "words . . . in the ear . . . of the mind." Words that,

> In the delicatest ear of the mind, repeat,
> Exactly, that which it wants to hear, at the sound
> Of which, an invisible audience listens,
> Not to the play, but to itself, expressed
> In an emotion as of two people, as of two
> Emotions becoming one.[16]

In just this way, it seems to me, the two languages harmonize in "Resolution and Independence."

BIBLIOGRAPHICAL NOTE

In their evaluations of Wordsworth's poetry, including "Resolution and Independence," Salvador de Madariaga and F. W. Bateson have derided the poet's bathetic voice ("The Case of

16 From "Of Modern Poetry," *The Collected Poems of Wallace Stevens* (New York, 1955), p. 240; by permission of Alfred A. Knopf, Inc.

Wordsworth" in *Shelly and Calderon* [London, 1920]; and *Wordsworth: A Re-Interpretation,* 2d ed. [London, 1956]. Stanley Edgar Hyman in *Poetry and Criticism* (New York, 1961) has illustrated the poem's "grandeur" along with "its terrible flatness" (p. 120). But W. W. Robson in his study, "Resolution and Independence" (1959; reprinted in his *Critical Essays* [New York, 1967], has found in it "the two contrasting aspects" of the poet himself, the prosaic and the visionary, which ultimately are reconciled in an "achieved integrity" (p. 132). Anthony E. M. Conran has revealed a "dialectic" between "ordinary life" and "revelation," the latter finally overcome by the former ("The Dialectic of Experience: A Study of Wordsworth's 'Resolution and Independence,' " *PMLA* 75 [1960]: 70). Albert S. Gérard has uncovered "contrapuntal variations" in patterns which incorporate the shifts in style (" 'A Leading from Above': Wordsworth's 'Resolution and Independence,' " pp. 121–124). And Geoffrey H. Hartman, sensitive to Wordsworth's uncertainties, has emphasized the "precarious intermingling of vision and matter-of-fact" in a lyric in which an "act of a living mind" lies "open to the terror of discontinuity" (*Wordsworth's Poetry,* p. 268).

[7]

Design in the
"Immortality Ode"

Two common assumptions are made about the meaning and structure of the "Immortality Ode." The first is that one can reason doubt into hope without any residuals— that growing up (an image for coming to terms with "reality") does not also imply growing old (an image for acknowledging loss or death). The second assumption is that stanzas four and five of the poem mark the transition between doubt and hope: that point in the poem where questioning— "Whither is fled the visionary gleam? / Where is it now, the glory and the dream?"—gives way to statement, "Our birth is but a sleep and a forgetting." It then follows from this assumption that the middle stanzas offer a first and tentative answer in the form of the myth of pre-existence and the fable of the growing child, and the last stanzas give the final and conclusive answer, the "faith" and "philosophic mind" of the mature poet.

However, if the poem is about growing up, it must also be about growing old; the two descriptions are but two views of the same process. Furthermore, the crucial point in the poem, its lowest ebb from which the poet must turn himself by an act of the will, comes at the end of the eighth stanza:

> Full soon thy Soul shall have her earthly freight
> And custom lie upon thee with a weight
> Heavy as frost and deep almost as life. [127–129]

Although the poet asks no formal question here, he sees that the very possibility of vision is "frozen" by custom, whether that vision be of past joy (I–IV) or of the joy of an imagined and pre-existent past (V–VIII). Frost bends the plants it falls upon with its weight; it also kills. The answer that follows, then, is an answer willed in the face of that frost.[1]

In support of this view we can turn to a suggestion made by Susanne Langer. In her book *Feeling and Form,* she stresses the process of thought as it is presented in poetry. She begins by describing "the occurrence of a thought" itself as "an event in a thinker's personal history" that has "as distinct a qualitative character as an adventure, a sight, or a human contact." Such an occurrence "is not a proposition,

---

[1] Jack Stillinger suggests this possibility in his edition of Wordsworth's *Selected Poems and Prefaces* (Boston, 1965), p. 538. An excellent essay by Florence G. Marsh, "Wordsworth's *Ode:* Obstinate Questionings," *Studies in Romanticism* 5 (1965–66): 219–230, shows a three-part structure working in the poem by comparing the form of the "Ode" with that of "Tintern Abbey" ("Ascent of the mount of vision, vision from the mount, and return to a more naturalistic level," p. 220). From a different perspective from mine, she too finds the first two sections (stanzas I–IV and V–VII) more in tune with each other than with the final section. Stuart M. Sperry, Jr., in "From 'Tintern Abbey' to the 'Intimations Ode': Wordsworth and the Function of Memory," *The Wordsworth Circle,* 1 (1970): 40–49, discusses the way memory works in the poem and in so doing strengthens the case for a three-part structure. Sperry is answered and his ideas extended by Kenneth R. Johnston in "Recollecting Forgetting: Forcing Paradox to the Limit in the 'Intimations Ode,'" in the same journal, 2 (1971): 59–64.

but the entertainment of one, which necessarily involves vital tensions, feelings, the imminence of other thoughts, and the echoes of past thinking." The poet, she reasons, is primarily concerned with the "occurrence of a thought," only secondarily with the thought itself.

Poetic reflections, therefore [she writes], are not essentially trains of logical reasoning, though they may incorporate fragments, at least of discursive argument. Essentially they create the semblance of reasoning, of the seriousness, strain and progress, the sense of growing knowledge, growing clearness, conviction and acceptance—the whole experience of philosophical thinking.[2]

For Wordsworth the experience brought great strain, a frequently halted progress, and a sharp sense of waning perception and brightness, of gnawing doubt and dejection. Sentence pattern and thematic development, intimately related throughout the poem, bear this antiphonal burden.

We shall see that the "semblance of reasoning" takes two basic forms, that which is clearly distinguishable as progressive, showing a "sense of growing knowledge, growing clearness, conviction and acceptance," to be found in the final three stanzas, and that which is remarkable for its eddying, unresolving / unresolvable movement and its dramatic moments of arrested motion, to be found in the first eight stanzas. Characteristic of the latter are sentence patterns of exploration and inquiry, of statement and counterstatement in uneasy balance, while in the former we find patterns of exclusion and assertion, of deliberative and argumentative process. I shall argue that this design is at one with the poem's thematic design: the primary thematic shift from doubt to conviction comes at the very point in the

2 New York, 1953, p. 219.

poem where the structural design, the way sentences and parts of sentences are built, makes its major turn.

I

If we examine how words and phrases are put together in the first eight stanzas we shall see at once that the sentence structures throughout these 130 lines are strikingly similar. In the manner of the short lyrics being written at the same time, the Butterfly poems, "To the Cuckoo," "The Sparrow's Nest," and others, these stanzas of the "Ode" build into units by accretion. The most frequent link is "and" (eleven times), the next most frequent is "but" (four times). The links involving more complex structures are noticeably scarce ("who," "which," "that," "though," and so on). Apart from simple counting, however, we note that each stanza is a subtle blend of the most basic, often paratactic, structures, and an occasional complex one.

Stanza one sets up the pattern of clausal repetition which is used to advantage throughout the first eight stanzas and then echoed with great effect in the tenth stanza. The first sentence, long but not complex, turns upon a "when" clause.

> There was a time *when* meadow grove and stream
> The earth and every common sight
>> To me did seem
> Apparel'd in celestial light
> The glory and the freshness of a dream.
>> [1–5; italics mine; so too below]

The repeated subject of the "when" clause, moving from particularity to inclusiveness, "meadow, grove, stream, earth, every common sight," is balanced after the verb "seem" by a doubled descriptive phrase, "celestial light" and its appositive, "the glory and the freshness of a dream." Internally, before the final balance is struck, "common sight" is set off against "celestial light." The next unit, "It *is not now* as it *has been* of *yore*," mirrors itself in the simplest of ways; while the third and last unit, more complex than the first two because of its initial modifying clause,

> Turn wheresoe'er I may
> By night or day

resolves itself into another repetition,

> The things which *I have seen I see* them now no more.
>
> [6–9]

Stanza two develops in a similar way except that the pattern is made simpler. The first five clauses are in effect sentences which stand by themselves, unjoined except for the first two which are linked by "and."

> The Rainbow comes and goes
> And lovely is the rose
> The moon doth with delight
> Look round her when the heavens are bare
> Waters on a starry night
> Are beautiful and fair
> The sunshine is a glorious birth. [10–16]

The direction in which the verse flows is skillfully reversed in the last unit (lines 17–18) at the turning phrase, "But yet," with a syntactic flourish in the forming of two short clauses followed by one of full line-length, the latter two subtly dependent on the first:

> But yet *I know* where'er *I go*
> That *there hath pass'd away a glory* from the earth.

This pattern is reversed in the third stanza, which begins with a comparatively involved structure:

> Now *while* the birds thus sing a joyous song
> And *while* the young lambs bound

As to the tabor's sound
To me alone *there came* a *thought* of grief
A timely *utterance gave* that thought *relief*
And *I again am strong.*   [19-24]

But as though to coincide with the "relief" of line 23 the verse slides back into near parataxis. Seven separate clauses follow, only three joined by "and."

The cataracts below their trumpets from the steep	(1)
No more shall grief of mine the season wrong	(2)
I hear the echoes through the mountains throng	(3)
The winds come to me from the fields of sleep	(4)
And all the earth is gay	(5)
Land and sea	
Give themselves up to jollity	(6)
And with the heart of May	
Doth every Beast keep holiday [25-33]	(7)

The repetition is doubled in the last clause for emphasis, as in a musical coda:

Thou Child of joy
Shout round me, let me hear thy *shouts thou* happy Shepherd *boy!*
[34-35]

The two apostrophes separated by the two verbal clauses form a pattern which suggests a sound and its echo, surrounded by a second sound and echo.

Stanza four returns to the pattern firmly established in stanza two, the movement from simple to complex, and embellishes it. The first five clauses (36-41) employ the device of repetition as their chief means to coherence.

Ye bless'd Creatures *I have heard* the call
Ye to each other make *I see*
The heavens laugh with you in your jubilee
My heart is at your festival

> My *head hath* its coronal
> Even yet more gladness *I can hold* it all. [36–41]

The later manuscript reads, "The fullness of your bliss, I feel—I feel it all." Wordsworth accentuated the iterative pattern in revision; here again the pattern is based upon pairs or doubling. The next unit (42–50) is psychologically complex and correspondingly reveals an involved sentence structure.

> [*It would be*]
> O evil day if *I were* sullen
> *While* the earth herself is adorning
> This sweet May morning
> *And* the children are pulling
> On every side
> In a thousand vallies far and wide
> Fresh flowers: *while* the sun shines warm
> *And* the Babe leaps up in his Mother's arm. [42–49]

Despite its complexity, notice that this much of the pattern is also based upon the principle of doubling. It is completed, however, with a triplet: "I hear I hear with joy I hear—". The final unit (51–57) begins dramatically with "But," and moves into a double image, "But there's a tree . . . A single field"; each image is modified by its own qualifying structure in an attempt to set it free of surrounding circumstances, "of many one . . . which I have looked upon." The two isolated images are then gathered up, "Both of them speak of something that is gone," and provided with a third image in which the concept of repetition is actually introduced:

> The pansy at my feet
> Doth the same tale *repeat*. [54–55]

Finally the stanza closes with two questions which echo one another:

Whither is fled the visionary gleam
Where is it gone the glory and the dream? [56–57]

The substantive, "gleam," divides and repeats itself as "the glory and the dream." The resonances are not only conceptual, in images of seeing and of light, or verbal, in repetitions of words that have occurred earlier, but syntactic as well. The device of doubling and the patterns created with it do not *mean* anything in themselves. Rather they are the linguistic mirrors of the poet's state of mind. Their eddying vacillation is like his, is at once the medium and the substance of his growing uncertainty.

That state of mind is borne out by the thematic development of the first four stanzas as they establish the basic conflict between "then" and "now" over which the poet broods. Stanza one begins in the past and states the loss; the second stanza recalls present scenes, what the poet is seeing "now"; but, paradoxically, this present glory is without "glory." In the third there is recompense in the power of the sounds of the present to delight. The "timely utterance" of lines twenty-two and twenty-three is framed in the past tense ("came" and "gave"), a use of that tense different from the real past of lines one to five. Unlike the earlier usage these verbs do not indicate a time before the fictional present of the poem (that is, before the time of the poet speaking). While those first lines describe a time clearly separated from the time of the poem ("there was a time"), the later lines are surrounded by the present moment, the "now," and come, deliberately I think, as a surprise (18–23).

This past tense is meant only to indicate a distinct interval or series of specific moments, one following upon the other, first the "thought of grief" then "the timely utterance" offering "relief," which are separate from the fictional present only in this verbal way. Phrasing it in what would seem the only alternative way makes this point clear. To say, "To me alone there *comes* a thought of grief / A timely utterance *gives* that thought relief," is to blur the momentary and sequential nature of the experience: all events seem simultaneous, indistinct and non-causal, merely part of that summary effect found often in Wordsworth's descriptive verse, and especially in the second stanza of this poem. There rainbow, rose, moon, waters, stars, sunshine, all seem to occur simultaneously, or at least do so to the poet's imagination. But the point of Wordsworth's phrasing in stanza three is to signal a change in tactics from the preceding stanza. The force of "now" is literal: Not "now-a-days" but "exactly at this moment." The utterance then cannot be a poem written earlier ("My heart leaps up"), nor even the portion of the rainbow poem written the day before but added as epigraph much later. Nor can it be the speech of the Leech-gatherer, as Lionel Trilling has proposed, which was recalled and written about after the "Ode" was begun. It may be, as E. D. Hirsch has argued, the first two stanzas of the "Ode" itself, spoken in "reverie," then recalled. But more likely, as the context shows, it is the very sounds that surround the poet "alone" in his grief, the trumpeting, echoing cataracts, the winds, and the shouts of the shepherd-boy.[3] This is important because the only compensations offered by stanzas one to four are the particular joys of the present moment. The

[3] H. W. Garrod (*Wordsworth* [Oxford, 1927]), seconded by John Crowe Ransom ("William Wordsworth: Notes toward an Understanding of Poetry," in *Wordsworth: Centenary Studies*, ed. G. T. Dunklin [Princeton, 1951], pp. 81–113), takes "My Heart Leaps Up" to be the "utterance." Trilling makes his suggestion in *Liberal Imagination*, pp. 138, 139; Hirsch makes his in *Wordsworth and Schelling*, pp. 150, 151. Hartman in *Wordsworth's Poetry* (p. 275) and Grob in "Wordsworth's 'Immortality Ode'" (p. 40) also suggest the surrounding sounds as a possible reading.

poet takes these pleasures, once they are offered (that is, noticed), by a nervous act of will. He describes and thus participates in the spontaneous beauty, the self-delight of the surrounding scene, but appeals subtly for its continuance, "Shout round me let me hear thy shouts" (35). In stanza four he reinforces his participation, by insistently repeating the personal pronouns and their accompanying verbs (36–41) as we noted above. He then scolds himself for responding sullenly to the Earth's adorning (42–43). And, finally, he reiterates his assertion of participation, "I hear I hear with joy I hear" (50).

It is essential to the poem's unity that the "philosophic mind" not be introduced too soon, as other attempts at identifying the "utterance" have made it necessary to do. For the "spots-of-time," the scenes called from memory at lines fifty and following, dispel the poet's willed effort and carry home the heart to unquietness, the very perplexity he had hoped to escape by plunging into the present moment (16–17, 56–57); but the past will not be put off, the old glories outshine the new.

As we have seen, the syntactic design of these first stanzas has been uniquely suited to the conveyance of their particular "semblance" of meditation. The design of the next four stanzas coincides in its sentence patterns with the first. Stanza five begins with a complex structure (lines 58–61) but one built upon the firmly established principle of doubling or pairing: the statement, "Our birth is but a sleep and a forgetting," itself containing pairing, is followed by a restatement in other terms, other images. Birth as sleep is redefined more richly if more ambiguously as the soul-star's second and more distant setting, distant, that is, from its first setting "elsewhere." What follows is a series of qualifying phrases or clauses, sometimes separated into distinct sentences, but nevertheless dependent on the opening statement. Each makes use of the doubling principle (italicized phrases). The first unit refers directly back to the first line in the stanza:

> *Not in* entire forgetfulness
> *And not in* utter nakedness
> *But* trailing clouds of glory do *we come*
> From God *who is* our home. [62–65]

The second, of simpler pattern, "heaven lies about us in our infancy" (66), is connected with the image of the soul as "our life's star" but echoes, too, the notion of "trailing clouds of glory." The third unit,

> *Shades* of the prison-house *begin to close*
> Upon the growing Boy
> But he *beholds* the light and whence it flows
> *He sees* it in his joy [67–70]

repeats the first term and qualifier (doubled) in the very language of light suggested earlier ("star" and "clouds of glory," where glory refers both to the child in his former greatness—the light of God upon him—and to the cloud touched by the rays of the sun when it is low in the sky).

The fourth unit,

> The *Youth who* daily farther from the East
> *Must travel,* still *is* Nature's Priest
> *And* by the vision splendid
> *Is* on his way *attended* [71–74]

echoes both sentence and image patterns, the latter in the acolyte whose calling and discipline make it necessary that he turn his back to the source of light, letting his journey through the world correspond with the sun's journey. Finally, in a development from this last image, but connected as well, by skillful repetition and variation as we have seen, with all the qualifiers and the original statement, the last lines of the stanza advance to the "man" who watches the vision *"die away / And fade* into the light of common day." The rocking pattern of statement and qualification, statement and qualification, built up from the basic pattern of doubling, is quietly brought to rest in simple terms and paratactic form.

Stanza six makes use of the structural variation developed in stanza three and refined in stanza five. Thematically it is an extension of the image of the soul-star which has "had elsewhere its setting" (60). "Setting" can mean either "descent" or "surroundings," the setting in which the soul-star had formerly lived or its gem-setting. The first reading is the more inviting because it is the more daring: the soul must die ("set") elsewhere before it can be born into this ordinary life. But in any case it is clear that ordinary life is where it has risen, the surroundings in which it finds itself, in the "lap" of Mother Earth. Earth is seen not as a mythological presence but as a well-meaning nurse, with dimly felt yearnings (for the star-life?), whose unwitting yet inevitable role is "to make her . . . Inmate Man / Forget the glories he hath known." The soul's experience of common day is rendered in terms of the foundling prince ("Foster child"), the simple, not unworthy peasant woman, and the imperial palace, all recognizable terms of children's fables.[4] Here in this ambiguous allegory, the sentence structure reflects the uncertainty:

> Earth fills her lap with pleasure of her own
> Yearnings she hath in her own natural kind
> And even with something of a Mother's mind
> And no unworthy aim
> The homely nurse doth all she can. [77–81]

[4] See Carl Woodring, *Wordsworth* (Boston, 1965), p. 92.

The way in which the qualifying parts of the sentence mount up before the main statement is made suggests a tentativeness, an uncertainty about the nurse herself, her motives and her deeds. Perhaps a look at one of Blake's prison-house images will make this clear. The chilling vision from "The Mental Traveller,"

> And if the Babe is born a Boy
> He's given to a Woman Old
> Who nails him down upon a rock
> Catches his shrieks in cups of gold, [9-12]

shows that for Blake there is no ambivalence about the "Mother" figure; she is simply malevolent from intention to act.[5] Wordsworth, however, is uncertain. But of course, whatever her motive, the final lines assert clearly that she is all too successful in making her charge forget; the doubling is especially obvious:

> The homely nurse doth all she can
> To make her *foster child* her *Inmate Man*
> *Forget* the *glories* he *hath known*
> *And* that imperial *palace* whence he *came*. [81-84]

After the fable, Wordsworth gives a naturalistic picture of the child's experience in the common day, a description of the child playing "grown-up" (the phrase "of a pigmy size," often mocked for its absurdity, is intended to be absurd: civilization's long fascination with the pygmy, with the unlikely hero, derives from the sharp jolt of incongruity he gives—a child's body harboring adult concerns). This stanza is also built by accretion and repetition rather than by argu-

[5] From *The Poetry and Prose of William Blake*, edited by David V. Erdman and Harold Bloom, copyright © 1965 by David V. Erdman and Harold Bloom. Reprinted by permission of Doubleday & Company, Inc.

ment. Each new detail becomes part of a picture in which the only sense of plot or movement is the impression of easy childish fluctuation from one imagined task to another. This effect of slight movement within a still frame is achieved by the device of listing several occupations in clusters, with plurality either made obvious or strongly implied:

> . . . some little plan *or chart* [90]

> A wedding *or* a festival
> A mourning *or* a funeral [93–94]

> Then will he fit his tongue
> To dialogues of business love *or* strife [97–98]

> Filling *from time to time* his humourous stage
> With *all* the *persons* down to palsied age
> That Life brings with her in her Equipage.
> [103–105]

Despite the multiplicity of childish "imitations," one sees the child as having descended into the heavy, almost fixed, but infinitely repeatable, dream (or "sleep") of ordinary human life. The doubling pattern, through its insistence on alternatives ("or" occurs four times in nine lines), reinforces this effect.

Stanza eight begins with an apparently elaborate, structurally complex statement. But it too breaks down into a simple series of apostrophes, repeated stabs at a definition, which come uncertainly to rest with the question "why."

> O Thou whose outward seeming doth belie
> Thy Soul's immensity
> Thou best philosopher who yet dost keep
> Thy heritage thou eye among the blind
> That deaf and silent read'st the eternal deep

Haunted for ever by the eternal mind
Thou mighty Prophet Seer blest
On whom those truth[s] do rest
Which we are toiling all our lives to find
O Thou on whom thy immortality
Broods like the day a Master o'er a Slave
A presence which is not to be put by
Thou unto whom the grave
Is but a lonely bed without the sense or sight
Of day or the warm light
A living place where we in waiting lie
Why with such earnest pains dost thou provoke
The years to bring the inevitable yoke
Thus blindly with thy blessedness at strife?

[108–126]

Earth, the homely nurse, will do her work, will bring joy
and pain, delight and sorrow, will weigh upon the soul
"full soon"; the frost of custom will reach nearly to the heart
("heavy as frost, and deep almost as life"). The long formation "Thou . . . Thou . . . Thou . . . Thou . . . Prophet . . . Seer . . . Thou . . . Thou . . . Why?" is a sign
of the poet's difficulty even in phrasing the question; it has
the same searching iterativeness as do the questions in
stanza four, in particular, and of the sentence pattern shown
to dominate the first seven stanzas, the same swaying movement from assertion to qualification and finally to question.
Such a pattern creates the greatest possible tension and implies the poet's difficulty in finding an answer.

This difficulty, reflected so clearly in the sentence patterns
of these stanzas, indeed of the whole poem up to this point,
is mirrored as well by the thematic conflicts between youth
and age developed in this section of the poem. The youth /
age antithesis, implicit in the poet's appeal to the shepherd
boy (35), is now localized in the image of the "growing boy."

The youth's journey in these stanzas runs roughly parallel with the journey of the Red Cross Knight in Book I of the *Faerie Queene*, a text which Wordsworth and his sister Dorothy had been reading together the night before the poet added some lines to the "Ode"[6] Even if there is no direct connection, it will help to talk of one in terms of the other. Each "child" starts in innocence and travels step by step into darkness; each hastens defeat by taking up the pleasures of Mother Earth (represented by Duessa in Spenser's poem); each is "imprisoned" in the world and by the worldly; ultimately each wins through to a philosophic mind, to a competence in reconciling lost innocence with the world as it is. Wordsworth, who is the youth he describes, does not reach this point until the closing three stanzas. There are indeed interesting similarities between Spenser's "tall clownish young man"[7] who presents himself before Gloriana with the plea that he be tested by "adventure," and Wordsworth's "four year's darling of a pigmy size," who "with such earnest pains dost . . . provoke / The years to bring the inevitable yoke / Thus blindly with [his] blessedness at strife" (86, 124–126). Like Red Cross, Wordsworth's "little child" puts on the "armor" of life, though admittedly not the armor of Christian life. Wordsworth's metaphor is from the theater; the "parts" conned by the "little Actor" from his elders, from "Life" herself, fill "his humorous stage / With all the persons down to palsied age" (102–107). Like Red Cross, the child is watched over by a female figure (both Mother Earth and his literal mother) but makes his way toward a comprehension of death by his own erring path.

[6] *DWJ*, 177.

[7] The letter to Sir Walter Raleigh. For a discussion of Wordsworth's use of "Spenserian" allegory in "Resolution and Independence" see Conran, p. 72, and Hartman, *Wordsworth's Poetry*, pp. 268–270.

These similarities point up some of the larger implications of Wordsworth's "traveller" image. The differences will make clear his own emphasis. Spenser understands the knight's "fall" as necessary and indeed fortunate (as was Adam's before him). Though Red Cross wishes to remain out of the world once he is introduced to the joys of divine meditation, the right choice is certainly to enter the world again, for there is ultimately the promise of union with Una when his journey is completed. Wordsworth, in making use of the allegory (if not Spenser's then the generalized Christian-Platonic one on which Spenser's depends), converts it to his own purpose. While the child's descent is necessary (that is, "inevitable"), it is not fortunate. And though Wordsworth speaks in the "Prospectus" to *The Excursion* of a unifying marriage, of the "blissful hour," yet he can only "sing in solitude," and in anticipation, "the spousal verse / Of this great consummation." [8] In this section of the "Ode" he is even less hopeful, expressing his mood, not without ambivalence, in images like the "prison-house" (67), the confined and confining "stage" (103), slavery (118), "the grave" (120), the "inevitable yoke" (125), and "frost" (129).

Stanza five, then, takes up the somber possibility already suggested in the closing lines of stanza four, stating it over in terms of myth; not as an alien element imported into the poem, though Wordsworth's own apology for it would so indicate,[9] but as an appropriate outgrowth of the child's

[8] *PW*, 5:4–5, ll. 56-57. These lines, originally written for "Home at Grasmere," may be as late as 1806. So John A. Finch has implied in "On the Dating of *Home at Grasmere*: A New Approach," in *Bicentenary Wordsworth Studies*, pp. 14–28. But see Jonathan Wordsworth's reservations on this question in his preface to the same book, pp. x–xi.

[9] *PW*, 4:463–464.

view of himself. The tone shifts in stanza six, becoming playful, mildly ironic. Earth is not the same thing as Nature —she is instead a "peasant-mother" or "homely nurse" who in doing her best sets the child on the journey away from "the glories he hath known." The nurse is treated gently (her aims are "not unworthy"), yet the view of the child's relation to his surroundings is an ironic one reminiscent of Romance: the sturdy, none-too-perceptive but good-hearted woman rears for her world the foundling prince who has come to her from quite another world. Like Duessa, in Spenser's poem, she threatens the hero; and like Una, somewhat doubtful of the outcome, she watches over her unpromising knight. Wordsworth's is a naturalistic allegory, really no more than an elaborated metaphor. It serves to reassert the dilemma of the first four stanzas, not to resolve it.

A further shift in tone occurs in the seventh stanza. While Earth's influence seemed inevitable and at least benign in intention, the picture of the child encouraged to play at the "darkness" of the adult world rather than the "light" of childhood is more nearly sardonic in effect. In the eighth stanza we return to the slower rhythms and the somber tones of the fifth stanza. Now the sober voice of age speaks to youth, who is the only keeper of "those truths" which age cannot win. Here the poet reflects sadly on the irony that youth eagerly seeks to play age's part, bringing on "the inevitable yoke," blindly at strife with blessedness. At this point the crisis is unresolved. The final image is of custom as a "frost" which is "deep almost as life"—that is, almost reaching the heart. This submerged but powerful image of the nearly frozen heart is crucial to the course the poem now takes. Our analysis of the first eight stanzas has shown Wordsworth to be at substantially the same impasse with the close of stanza eight as he was with that of four. The two units, one through four and five through eight, are structurally and thematically of one piece—theme and variation. Contrary to the traditional view that places the crisis at the fourth and fifth stanzas, the sharpest turn is to be found at the present juncture, at stanzas eight and nine.

II

In the final stanzas the pattern changes. As we might expect, the structural coherence of stanzas one through eight, shaped from the consistent, though varied, use of the basic patterns of doubling and alternation, is not carried over into the final three stanzas since it is no longer the appropriate instrument. The answer provided by stanza nine is the compensation of memory, the "something that doth live" untouched by the deepening frost of custom—memory not of "Delight and liberty" but of "obstinate questionings," "vanishings," "misgivings," "instincts," and "those first affections / Those shadowy recollections" (131–146, and later variants). Here the language and its patterning become extraordinarily difficult, built up from simple units, but logically rather than accretively, in a long series of dependent formations. The introductory four lines, a single sentence with three clauses, leads to a simply phrased statement,

> The thought of our past years in me doth breed
> Perpetual benedictions;

but the following clause, which is itself rich in dependent structures, is what carries the weight of the argument for recompense.

> *Not* indeed
> *For that* which is most worthy to be blest
> Delight and liberty the simple creed

Of childhood whether fluttering or at rest
With new-born hope forever in his breast,
 Not for these I raise
 The song of thanks and praise
But for those [obstinate questionings
Of sense and outward things,
Fallings from us, vanishings;
Blank] [10] misgivings of a Creature
Moving about in worlds not realized
High instincts before which our mortal nature
Did tremble like a guilty thing surprized
 But for those first affections
 Those shadowy recollections
 Which be they what they may
Are yet the fountain light of all our day
Are yet the master light of all our seeing
 Uphold us *cherish* us and *make*
Our noisy years seem moments in the being
Of the eternal silence truths that wake
 To perish never
Which neither listlessness *nor* mad endeavour
 Nor Man *nor* Boy,
Nor all that is at enmity with joy
Can utterly abolish *or* destroy. [135–158]

Repetition is part of the formal pattern (indicated by italics). But it is no longer used to create the semblance of querulousness, of the poet's wavering state of mind. Instead it is used to build that "semblance of reasoning" which, as Professor Langer has said, can show a "sense of growing knowledge, growing clearness, conviction and acceptance." It is the syntax of careful exclusion and assertion rather than of accretive doubling or of statement and counterstatement. This semblance of a deliberative and argumentative process is a

[10] Not in MS M (1804), but found in L (1806–1807).

marked change in register. The shift comes about by an act of will, an act signalled by the poet's adopting a different way of shaping his experience linguistically.

With startling effect, then, stanza ten returns to the bounding lambs and singing birds of the opening stanzas. And to signal this return, the poet echoes the accretive pattern of those early stanzas:

> Then *sing ye* Birds *sing sing* a joyous *song*
> And let the young lambs bound
> As to the Tabor's sound!
> We in thought will join your throng
> *Ye that pipe* and *ye that play*
> *Ye that* through your hearts today
> *Feel* the gladness of the May. [166–171]

But a new stance qualifies the promise, "We *in thought* will join your throng." For "thought" also contains the knowledge that the light is gone. And it is at this point precisely that the argumentative pattern re-establishes itself:

> What though it be past the hour [11]
> *Of* splendour in the grass, *of* glory in the flower,
> *We will* grieve *not, rather* find
> Strength *in* what remains behind;
> [*In* the primal sympathy
> *Which* having been must ever be;] [12]
> *In* the soothing thoughts *that* spring
> Out of human suffering;
> *In* the faith *that* looks through death;
> *In* years *that* bring the philosophic mind. [172–179]

[11] The later MS reads:

> *What though* the radiance *which* was once so bright
> Be now for ever taken from my sight,
> *Though* nothing can bring back the hour.

[12] Added to the later MSS.

134

After the initial echo with its clue to change, the remainder of stanza ten is framed in the careful language of assessment and exclusion signaled by the instruments of sequential discourse.

The final stanza is both a prayer to Nature to keep the bonds unsevered and an exquisitely turned statement of the way things now stand.

> And Oh! ye fountains meadows fields & groves
>   Think not of any severing of our loves
>
> Yet in my heart of hearts I feel your might
>
>   I only have relinquished one delight
>   To live beneath your more habitual sway;
>
> I love the brooks which down their channels fret,
>   Even more than when I tripped lightly as they
>   The innocent brightness of a new-born day
>   Is lovely yet
> The clouds that gather round the setting sun
> Do take a sober colouring from an eye
> That hath kept watch o'er mans mortality
> Another race hath been, and other palms are won
>
>   Thanks to the human heart by which we live
>   Thanks to its tenderness its joys and fears
>   To me the meanest flower that blows can give
>   Thoughts that do often lie too deep for tears.

[180–197]

Some of the tensions and anxieties remain: Nature's might is felt, but one delight at least has been sacrificed; the "innocent brightness of a new born day / Is lovely yet," but the poet's innocence, he implies, is relinquished. The clouds now are sober-hued to an eye educated by knowledge of death. The structural arrangement, as indicated by the spacing, settles into units of one, two, three, and four pentameter lines (broken by a single short line), nearly every statement made in terms of a simple image. Any one statement could in itself conclude the poem; there is no real advance of thought in these final lines. Rather the poet abandons the device of argument as he did the earlier device of playfully yet seriously alternating image with counter-image. We have instead here at the close a gathering of sedate and measured statements, spoken in the register of acceptance and conviction.

Just as the poet's sentence structures shift radically in design in these final stanzas, so the thematic changes are large and profound. At stanza nine coincident with the shift in syntactic structure, the tone goes through not so much a shift as a sharp reversal. We return to "joy" (the concern of the third and fourth stanzas); but now the source of joy is not in the present scene, nor is it in the past scene and its remembered "liberties" and "delights," but rather in the act of memory itself:

> O joy that in our embers
> Is something that doth live
> That nature yet remembers
> What was so fugitive. [130–133]

By "nature" Wordsworth now seems to mean "human nature" or the natural condition; the metaphor of the living embers carries the prose sense home with great force, suggesting the awareness of a loss which is nearly disguised by the apostrophe: the glowing embers are but a pale "memory" of the fire that once was. The poet is thankful for an act of mind in the child (an "intimation of immortality," 142ff.), which is characterized both by "questionings" and by "recollections." This act of mind, both experiential and reflective, breeds in the poet "perpetual benediction" (135). It is still, now captured by adult memory, "the fountain light of all our day . . . the master light of all our seeing" (149–150).

Wordsworth finds in this act of mind the power to turn "our noisy years" into "moments in the being / Of the eternal silence," and these moments into "truths that wake / To perish never" (152–154). The feverish denial in the next lines indicates the strength of the oppressors, bringing the stanza to a bright loud climax. But with faultless timing Wordsworth comes gently down from this height by means of the justly famous and very beautiful image of calling back:

> Hence in a season of calm weather
> Though inland far we be
> Our souls have sight of that immortal sea
>   Which brought us hither
> Can in a moment travel thither
> And see the children sport upon the shore
> And hear the mighty waters rolling evermore.
>
>   [159–165]

This passage has a double function. First, it brings the crescendo of stanza nine to a quiet close. And second, the image like no other in the poem attempts to satisfy the need established by the poem's argument for a fusion of past and present rather than a mere assertion of such a union. The poet introduces the images from the first four stanzas, which then had brought joy only by an act of will and had really led, despite the poet's efforts, to a full sense of separation and loss, a loss allegorized and dramatized in the second four stanzas. Now, however, though the images are unified by memory into a momentary single vision,[13] he explicitly acknowledges his distance "inland," his separation. He is content

[13] See Bloom, *Visionary Company*, pp. 172, 173.

now to *see* "in a moment," having relinquished his earlier desire for participation through an endless present. And momentary that vision is. The only direction appropriate to the poem now is descent. Stanza ten is a verbal as well as structural echo of stanza three, but as we noted earlier the tone is changed, the separation is an acknowledged fact. Now, out of his second act of will (a wiser, more mature, but more melancholy act than the first) the poet accepts the recompense in what is left—"the philosophic mind." In stanza eleven the poet insists he still feels the "might of Nature" though he fears the "severing of our loves" (181–182). From the new stance of the philosophic mind, he endeavors to lessen, or at least to compensate for, the loss. But as he names the compensations one is conscious of a set of more brilliant images, of which these are mere reflections: the brook, the sunrise, the clouds gathering round the setting sun, reflections of those hard bright scenes of the opening stanzas which the poet willed his heart to enter. There was brilliance, here are the pale remains. "Another race" than the one he might have run "hath been"; "other palms" than the ones he might have won "are won" (192). In other words, "It is not now as it hath been of yore" (6). The final lines pay tribute to the human heart, its tenderness and joys (it does not freeze after all) but do not omit its fears and sadness. It has not frozen, but neither has it been fully warmed in the sun. Growing up and growing old are the same.

III

I have sought to demonstrate in this chapter how Wordsworth conveys the semblance of reasoning in all its experiential variousness and richness and drama. In so doing I have purposely shifted the emphasis away from a strict consideration of the content of the poem's argument, as though it were a "train of logical reasoning," and have attempted instead an appraisal of its manner as well as its matter. My view of the poem's design, then, reveals a poetics in which form and substance are one, in which the theme stated and the pattern of statement are fused. I see it, in Wallace Stevens' phrase, as a "poem of the mind in the act of finding / What will suffice." [14] Although part of the poem was not written until 1804, it nevertheless represents the culmination of the poet's experiments in the "lyric spirit of philosophy" during the spring of 1802.

BIBLIOGRAPHICAL NOTE
Critics have, for the most part, assumed a two-part structure in the poem. G. Wilson Knight, *The Starlit Dome* (London, 1941), 37–49, focusing on the image of the child, sees the "vital centre" of the poem in the ninth stanza but "the central towering height" in the sixth, what he later calls "the fiery heart" to which the beginning and end are "outer rose-petals" (p. 48). When Knight sees the poem "spatially," he sees it as problem (I–IV), solution (V–VIII), and conclusion (IX–XI—"and so the ode dims to a noble conclusion"—p. 48). This is essentially a two part division, with the crucial "turn" coming at stanza five. Cleanth Brooks, "Wordsworth and the Paradox of the Imagination," in *The Well Wrought Urn* (London, 1949, 1968), 101–123, has shown how the images of the early stanzas prepare for stanzas five and nine, and how stanza nine attempts a "recovery." The solution, Brooks feels, is "asserted rather than dramatized" (p. 121), and he is confused and disappointed by the

[14] The opening lines of the poem "Of Modern Poetry," *The Collected Poems of Wallace Stevens* (New York, 1955), p. 239; by permission of Alfred A. Knopf, Inc.

poem's vagueness. His difficulty seems to have arisen from his underlying assumption that the poem is, or ought to be, an argument not unlike the one outlined by Knight. Lionel Trilling, in *The Liberal Imagination* (pp. 129–153), divides the poem into three main parts, question (I–IV), first answer ("resistance," V–VIII), and second answer ("acceptance," IX–XI). E. D. Hirsch, in "Both-and Logic in Wordsworth's 'Immortality Ode,' " *Wordsworth and Schelling* (New Haven, 1960), carefully disavows biographical evidence but splits the poem in the traditional way (p. 148). Harold Bloom's division of parts in *The Visionary Company* (London, 1961) is very similar to Trilling's (p. 167). Geoffrey H. Hartman in *Wordsworth's Poetry* speaks provocatively, but briefly, of the poem's *"style* of thought" but falls back upon the classical terms for describing the ode form. The "stand" comes at stanza five where "the passion seems to level out into a new generalization or withdrawal from personal immediacy" (pp. 273, 274). However, in *Unmediated Vision* (New Haven, 1954), Hartman makes some general comments, based on "Tintern Abbey," which have bearing on the "Ode" and my discussion of it. In speaking of Wordsworth's imagination, he says that "Wordsworth's understanding is characterized by the general absence of the will to attain relational knowledge, that is, knowledge which may be obtained in direct answer to the Why, the What, the Wherefore, and the How" (p. 5). He speaks elsewhere, too, of the "act of will" (pp. 15–20) , but does not apply these insights directly to the "Ode." Alan Grob, in "Wordsworth's 'Immortality Ode' and the Search for Identity," bases his argument firmly on the assumption that only the first four stanzas were composed in 1802: the "basic materials of 1802 undergo in 1804 a substantial shift in function, transposed from literal facts of perception into broad epistemological metaphors" (p. 53). For views similar to mine, see n. 1, above.

The following studies of syntax in poetry have been found variously helpful or provocative: G. Rostrevor Hamilton, *The Tell-Tale Article* (New York, 1950); Donald Davie, *Articulate Energy* (London, 1955); Francis Berry, *Poet's Grammar* (London, 1958); Samuel R. Levin, *Linguistic Structures in Poetry* (The Hague, 1962); J. P. Thorne, "Stylistics and Generative Grammars," *Journal of Linguistics* 1 (1965): 49–59; Levin, "Internal and External Deviation in Poetry," *Word* 21 (1965): 225–237; William E. Baker, *Syntax in English Poetry, 1870–1930* (Berkeley and Los Angeles, 1967); William O. Hendricks, "Three Models for the Description of Poetry," *Journal of Linguistics* 5 (1969): 1–22. The linguists have often been drawn to the individual poem in recent years. But most grammatical analyses of literature that have appeared have been concerned either with "deep structure" (especially with matters of deletion) or else with the metrical qualities of "surface structure." Linguists have not yet developed a vocabulary for discussing, in ways they would accept as "precise," such devices as "doubling" or "repetition" or "reversal." When I speak of these matters as elements of syntax or sentence structure I refer to the patterns of words that actually occur and recur throughout the poem, not to underlying formatives or rules that determine the unique structure of each sentence.

Donald Davie in the work cited understands "syntax" in broad terms, as I do. In his treatment of the Romantics, he finds that they give syntax "only a phantasmal life in poetry." Wordsworth and poets after him, Davie says, have assumed "that when syntactical forms are retained in poetry those forms can carry no weight" (pp. 61, 63). But Davie later describes, as one of five varieties, a "subjective syntax," the function of which "is to please us by the fidelity with which it follows the 'form of thought' in the poet's mind" (p. 68). Another variety is "syntax like music" the function of which is "to please us by the fidelity with which it follows a 'form of thought' through the poet's mind *but without defining that thought*" (p. 86). We are reminded by Davie that "thought" is meant to include the experience or feeling of thought. In describing a "syntax like music," he coincides with Susanne Langer's view that "poetic reflections . . . essentially . . . create the *semblance* of reasoning" (*Feeling and Form* [New York, 1952], p. 219). Professor Langer's prime ex-

141

ample for her analysis is Wordsworth's use of the doctrine of transcendental remembrance in the "Ode." The idea does not go beyond the poem, according to Professor Langer; it serves to convey "depth of experience rather than depth of thought" (p. 220). As I argue here in this section, Professor Langer's phrase "the semblance of reasoning" can best be understood if applied to the whole poem where the "semblance" itself goes through important transformations. One could say, perhaps, that the poet shifts from a syntax like music in the first eight stanzas to a subjective syntax in the last three. At this level of abstraction the terms seem not very helpful.

PART II

THE POEMS

Introduction

My aim in including these poems has been to provide a convenient text of the "finished" versions as they stood in 1802, before Wordsworth's extensive revisions preparatory to the publication of *Poems in Two Volumes* in 1807 and the many collected editions thereafter. My method has been to seek out the manuscript version for each poem that can be dated closest to the spring of 1802, the time of composition. In some cases 1802 manuscripts are lacking, making it necessary to consult those of 1803, 1804 and 1806–1807. In one instance the poem "Travelling" became part of a longer poem composed many years later, but some lines of which were written perhaps four years before 1802; I have given the poem as it stands in the manuscript of 1802. In another instance, the "Immortality Ode," the poem was not completed until two years after it was begun; however, to avoid unnecessary confusion, I have given all of the "Ode" as we find it in the manuscript of 1804.

The chief manuscripts, in chronological order, are:

"Sara Hutchinson's Poets" (SHP) is a notebook anthology of poems principally by Wordsworth and Coleridge kept by Sara Hutchinson in 1802 and after. The evidence of the manuscript suggests that all but one of the poems by Wordsworth were copied into the notebook during the spring of 1802. This manuscript is now at Dove Cottage Library, Grasmere.[1]

Manuscript M of *The Prelude,* or Verse 25 of the Dove Cottage Papers, is a collection of poems evidently prepared for Coleridge to take with him on leaving England in April 1804. The manuscript contains fair copies of *The Prelude, The Ruined Cottage, Peter Bell,* and a gathering of poems

[1] The manuscript has been described and the Coleridge poems transcribed by George Whalley, *Coleridge and Sara Hutchinson and the Asra Poems* (Toronto, 1955). Helen Darbishire provides a partial transcription of the Wordsworth poems in her revision of *Poems in Two Volumes 1807,* 2d ed. (Oxford, 1952), pp. 471–482. The same material appears in *PW,* 2:535–543, but not in the same order as in the MS. S. H. leads off the notebook with the title "Sara Hutchinson's Poets." C.'s poems, ranging in date of composition from 1799 to 1812, occupy the next twelve leaves. But S. H. reversed the book to begin W.'s poems. The twenty-three poems of 1802 follow in close order in the MS, taking up the first nineteen and the recto of the twentieth leaves. Each page is numbered by the transcriber from 1 to 31 through the twenty-second poem (I count "These chairs" and "I have thoughts" as one poem). The top of leaf 18 has been cut away and the poem "A Farewell" begins leaf 19 but without numbering. (The section cut away appears to have been a false start in copying "A Farewell.") The next poem, not by W., begins on the verso of leaf 20. After this poem, on the verso of leaf 23, S. H. has transcribed W.'s "Praise be the Art, whose subtle power could stay" (1811). The next twenty leaves of the notebook are blank, except for some writing in pencil, perhaps in S. H.'s hand, that has been erased (29 verso to 31 recto). Since one of the poems, S. H.'s version of "Resolution and Independence," must have been copied into the notebook between 9 May and 14 June 1802 (see *DWJ,* 158, 159, and *EY,* 1:364–367), the contemporaneity of the W. poems, "Praise be" excepted, is strongly suggested. Those poems that may have been written in 1802 are surrounded in the MS by those that certainly were written then. The poem from 1811 occurs last in the MS after the sequence had been broken with the album piece by an unknown author ("P. M. J." of Birmingham).

composed between 1800 and 1804, all but a few of which were published in *Poems* (1807). It seems virtually certain that the short poems in this group were all composed by March or April of 1804, when the Wordsworths were preparing the transcripts to send to Coleridge before his departure for Malta.[2]

Manuscript L is the Longman MS of *Poems in Two Volumes* that was sent piecemeal to the printer in 1806–1807. It contains all the poems printed in 1807, many of which vary significantly from the printed versions. This manuscript is in the British Museum.[3]

The manuscript of "Resolution and Independence" sent to Sir George Beaumont by Coleridge on August 13, 1803, is the earliest transcription extant of the second version of the poem. This letter, in Coleridge's hand, is among the Coleorton Papers (MA 1581) in The Pierpont Morgan Library.[4] For purposes of easy comparison, the text found in this MS is presented below, not in chronological order, but

[2] See *EY*, 1:458–459, D. W. to Catherine Clarkson, 25 March 1804, and Moorman, 2:10; *EY*, 1:594, W. W. to Sir George Beaumont, 3 June 1805, where he says that he has "finished" his "Poem." See also Helen Darbishire's account of MS M in *Prel*, pp. xxx–xxxi; Jonathan Wordsworth's rebuttal in *The Music of Humanity*, p. 165, n. 2; and Mark L. Reed's presentation of convincing new evidence that links MS M to C. in a review of Wordsworth's book, *JEGP* 69 (1970): 532–533. As Wordsworth and Reed point out, however, the puzzle of S. H.'s autograph transcriptions in a MS prepared during her absence from Grasmere goes unsolved.

[3] *MY*, 2:145, W. W. to Lady Beaumont, 21 May 1807. The Longman MSS were described in W. H. White, *A Description of the Wordsworth and Coleridge Manuscripts in the Possession of Mr. T. Norton Longman* (London, 1897).

[4] *STCL*, 2:966–970. See also B. Ifor Evans' transcription in *Modern Language Review*, 16 (1951): 355–358. My own transcription differs in minor details both from Griggs's and from Brown's.

on facing pages with the text of "The Leech-Gatherer" from SHP. I am pleased to express my thanks to the trustees of Dove Cottage, the British Museum, and The Piermont Morgan Library for granting me permission to publish the material from their respective collections. "The Barberry-Tree," first published in the *New Statesman*, 31 July 1964, has been transcribed from a photocopy of the MS, courtesy of Christ Church Library; and permission to publish has been granted by The Governing Body of Christ Church, Oxford.[5]

In the headnotes for each poem I have given the dates of composition and publication, the evidence for the former, the manuscript source, and the location in *The Poetical Works*.

I have given titles as they appear in the manuscripts. A title, or for that matter any phrasing in the text itself, that is supplied from another source appears in brackets. This source is identified in the footnotes. I have also used brackets to indicate a torn or otherwise illegible manuscript. Again, reasonable conjectures about missing words or lines are supplied from other sources and are so identified in the footnotes.

In every case I have transcribed the text from a single manuscript, the earliest finished text available, with any minor departures from this rule indicated. The arrangement is chronological, those poems that can be precisely dated appearing first, then poems that can be assigned certainly but only generally to the spring of 1802, and finally poems probably written then but about which there is some doubt.

[5] See also Jonathan Wordsworth's "The New Wordsworth Poem," *College English* 27 (1966): 456–458.

Editorial Conventions

[dwell], Jaco[b]	material in brackets supplied by editor
[?fain]	doubtful reading
[ ]	gap in manuscript
del.	bracketed word, phrase, or line has been deleted
del. from	than *del. from* then "then" has been deleted and corrected to "than"
illeg.	illegible
interlined	material has been written between the original lines of the text, usually as a substitute for a deleted word or phrase, sometimes to supply a missing line or word
orig.	original
reinstated	deleted word subsequently reinstated
supplied	material inserted by the editor from a specified source

The title is from MS L; D. W. refers to it as "The Singing Bird" in 1802 (*DWJ*, 130). Composed 11 and 12 March 1802 (*DWJ*, 130, 131); published in 1807. Source: SHP (see *PW*, 2:54, 55, 538).

The day was cold and rain and wet;
A foggy day in winter time,
—A Woman in the road I met
Not old, though something past her prime;
—Majestic seem'd she as a mountain storm;   5
A Roman Matron's gait—like feature & like form

The ancient spirit is not dead;
Old times thought I, are breathing there;
Proud was I that my country bred
Such strength, a dignity so fair,   10
—She begg'd an alms, like one of low estate;
I look'd at her again, nor did my pride abate.

When from my lofty thoughts I woke,
With the first word I had to spare
I said to her, "Beneath your cloak   15
What is it you are carrying there?"
She answer'd soon as she the question heard,
"A simple Burthen Sir, a little singing Bird!"

"My eldest Son, a Sailor, sail'd
"With God's good blessing many a day   20
"But at the last, his fortune fail'd—
"—In Denmark he was cast away:
"At Hull he liv'd where I have been to see
"What clothes he might have left, or other property.

"The room in which he lodg'd was small,   25
"And few effects were in it, when

"I reach'd the place; I sold them all,
"And now am travelling home again.
"I live at Mary-port, a weary way!
"And scarcely what I have will for my journey pay.　　30

"The Bird and cage they both were his,
" 'Twas my Son's Bird;—and neat and trim
"He kept it—many voyages
"This singing-bird hath gone with him;
"And I, God help me! for my little wit　　35
"Trail't with me, Sir! he took so much delight in it! "

[ALICE FELL]

The title is from D. W.'s journal of 1802 (*DWJ*, 131) and MS M. Composed 12 and 13 March 1802 (*DWJ*, 131); published in 1807. Source: SHP (see *PW*, 1:232–234; 2:542).

[   ]

The sky grows wild—a storm is near   5
Clouds gather and the moon is drown'd—
What is it that strange sound I hear?
What is the meaning of that sound?

As if the wind blew many ways
I hear the noises more and more;   10
—Down go the windows of the chaise,
And the noise follows as before.

"Hola! what noise is that," said I,
The Post Boy halted at the word
I listened, neither voice nor cry   15
Nor aught else like it could be heard.

The Post Boy smack'd his whip, and fast
The horses scamper'd through the rain;
And as before between the blast
I heard the self same sound again.   20

[Said I alighting on the ground,
What can it be this piteous moan
And there a little Girl I found
Sitting behind the Chaise alone]

1–4 *MS torn away.*
21–24 *MS torn away. Supplied from MS M. There may have been another stanza in SHP.*

" 'Tis torn in pieces look!—look here[!"]   25
Entangled in the wheel it hung,
A weather-beaten rag as e'er
Upon a murderer's gibbet hung.

'Twas twisted between nave and spoke
She lent her help—and with good heed   30
Together we releas'd the Cloak
A wretched wretched rag indeed!

"Whither are you going, Child?
To night along these lonesome ways?"
"To Durham" a[n]swer'd she half wild,   35
"Then come with me into the chaise."

She sate like one past all relief,
Sobs after sobs she forth did send
In misery, as if her grief
Could never never have an end.   40

"My Child in Durham do you dwell?"
She check'd herself in her distress
And said "my name is Alice Fell,
I'm fatherless, and motherless.

And I to Durham, Sir, belong"   45
And then as if the thought would choke
Her very heart, her grief grew strong
And all was for her tatter'd cloak

The chaise drove on—our journeys end
Was nigh, and sitting by my side   50
As if she'd lost her only Friend
She wept, nor would be pacified.

Up to the Tavern-door we post,
Of Alice and her grief I told

25 in *del. from* to

And I gave money to the host   55
To buy a new cloak for the old.

"And let it be of duffel grey
As warm a cloak as man can sell"
Proud Creature was she the next day
The little Orphan Alice Fell.—   60

The title is from MS L; D. W. refers to it in 1802 as "The Beggar Woman" and "The Beggar Boys" (*DWJ*, 131, 132). Composed 13 and 14 March 1802 (*DWJ*, 131, 132); published in 1807. Source: SHP (see *PW*, 2:222–224, 539).

She had a tall man's height or more;
No bonnet screen'd her from the heat;
A long drab-coloured cloak she wore,
A mantle reaching to her feet:
What other dress she had I could not know   5
Only she wore a cap that was as white as snow.

In all my walks through field or town,
Such figure never had I seen:
Her face was of Egyptian brown;
Fit person was she for a queen   10
To head those Ancient Amazonian files
Or ruling Banditt's wife among the Grecian Isles

Before me begging she did stand,
Pouring out sorrows like a sea
Grief after grief. On English land   15
Such woes thought I can never be!
—"And yet some small assistance you shall have
And for your beauty's sake—you are a woman brave"

Second Part

I left her and pursued my way:
And soon, before me, did I spy   20
A pair of little Boys at play,

4 reaching *interlined.*   15 *interlined.*

Chasing a crimson butterfly:
The elder followed with his hat in hand
Wreathed round with yellow flowers the gayest of the land

They spied me all at once—and lo!   25
Each ready with a plaintive whine!
"Not more than half an hour ago
Your mother has had alms of mine"
"That could not be" said one "my mothers dead"
"Nay but I gave her pence and she will buy you bread"   30

"She has been dead Sir, many a day"
"Sweet Boys you're telling me a lie
It was your mother as I say."—
And in the twinkling of an eye,
"Come, come," said one, and without more ado   35
Off to some other play they both together flew.

Composed 14 March 1802 (*DWJ*, 132); published in 1807. Source: SHP. There is a transcription of this poem and "The Sparrow's Nest" in a letter from C. to Thomas Poole, 7 May 1802 (*STCL*, 2:801), but the letter gives a later version. (See *PW*, 1:226; 2:541.)

Stay near me! do not take thy flight!
A little moment stay in sight!
Much reading do I find in thee;
Thou Bible of my infancy!
Float near me—do not yet depart!   5
Dead times revive in thee;
Thou bring'st gay creature as thou art,
A solemn image to my heart,
My Father's family!

O! pleasant, pleasant, were the days   10
The time when in our childish plays,
My sister Dorothy and I
Together chased the Butterfly.
A very hunter I did rush
Upon the prey:—with leaps and springs   15
I followed on from brake to bush:
—But she, God love her! fear'd to brush
The dust from off his wings.

18 *William Heath conjectures that the two Butterfly poems were originally one, basing his case mainly on the physical appearance of the poems in MS L. However their inclusion as separate poems here and again in MS M would seem to undermine his argument (Wordsworth and Coleridge, pp. 59–64).*

Composed 16 and 17 March 1802 (*DWJ*, 133, 135); published in 1807. Source: SHP (see *PW*, 2:56–59, 538).

Dear Babe! thou daughter of another
One moment let me be thy mother!
An infant's face and looks are thine,
And sure a mother's heart is mine.
Thy own dear mother's far away   5
At labour in the harvest field,
Thy little sister is at play;
What warmth and comfort would it yield
To my poor heart if thou couldst be
One little hour a Child to me!   10

Across the waters I am come,
And I have left a Babe at home;
A long long way of land & sea!
Come to me, I'm no Enemy!
I am the same who at thy side   15
Sate yesterday, and made a nest
For thee sweet baby! thou has tried
Thou know'st the Pillow of my breast.
Good, good art thou, alas to me
Far more than I can be to thee!   20

Here little Darling! dost thou lie,
An infant thou a mother I.
Mine wilt thou be—thou hast no fears
Mine are thou—spite of these my tears—
Alas before I left the spot,   25
My Baby and its dwelling place
The nurse said to me tears should not

20 than *del. from* then

Be shed upon an infants face
It was unlucky—no—no—no—
No truth is in them who say so.   30

My own dear Harry he will sigh
Sweet Babe! and they will let him die.
"He pines" they'll say "it is his doom,
And you may see his day is come."
Oh! had he but thy chearful smiles   35
Limbs stout as thine, and lips as gay,
These looks, thy cunning and thy wiles
And countenance like a summer's day,
They would have hopes of him, and then
I should behold his face again.   40

'Tis gone—forgotten—let me do
My best—there was a smile or two—
I can remember them, I see
The smiles worth all the world to me
Dear Baby! I must lay thee down;   45
Thou troublest me with sore alarms,
Smiles hast thou sweet ones of thy own,
—I cannot keep thee in my arms
For they confound me—as it is
I have forgot those two of his.   50

Oh! how I love thee! we will stay
Together here this one half-day.
My sister's child who bares my name,
From France across the ocean came
She with her mother cross'd the Sea;   55
The Babe and mother near me dwell;
My darling! she is not to me
What thou art, though I love her well;
Rest, little Stranger! rest thee here—
—Never was any Babe more dear   60

56 mother [dwell *del.*] near me dwell

160

Composed around 23 to 26 March 1802 (*DWJ*, 137, 138) but worked on perhaps as late at 14 May (*DWJ*, 161) or even 3 June (*DWJ*, 168, 169); published in 1807. Source: SHP (see *PW*, 2:207, 208, 539).

O blithe new-comer I have heard
I hear thee and rejoice:
O Cuckoo shall I call thee bird
Or but a wandering voice?

While I am lying on the grass   5
I hear thy hollow shout
From hill to hill it seems to pass
About & all about.

To me no Babbler with a tale
Of sunshine and of showers   10
Thou tellest Cuckoo in the vale
Of visionary hours.

Thrice welcome, darling of the spring!
Ev'n yet thou art to me
No Bird, but an invisible thing,   15
A voice, a mystery

The same who in my school-boy days
I listen'd to, whom I
Look'd for a thousand thousand ways
In bush, and tree, & sky   20

To seek thee did I often rove
Through woods & on the green
And thou wert still a hope a love
Still long'd for never seen.

And I can listen to thee yet
Can lie upon the plain
And listen till I do beget
That golden time again.

25

O blessed Bird! the earth we pace
Again appears to be
An unsubstantial fairy place
That is fit home for thee.

30

The title is found only in SHP; D. W. calls it "The Rainbow" (*DWJ,* 139, 162). Composed 26 March 1802 (*DWJ,* 139) but worked on again 14 May (*DWJ,* 162); published in 1807. Source: SHP (see *PW,* 1:226; 2:541).

My heart leaps up when I behold
A Rainbow in the sky:
So was it when my life began;
So is it, now I am a man,
So be it, when I shall grow old   5
Or let me die!
The Child is Father of the man;
And I should wish that all my days may be
Bound each to each by natural Piety.

[ODE]

The title is from MS L; D. W. refers to it simply as "an ode" (*DWJ*, 139). Part of the poem was composed 27 March, and W. worked on it again 17 June 1802 (*DWJ*, 177). No doubt the first four stanzas were written during this period, as W. himself stated in the IF note to the poem. But it is still problematical whether any more stanzas were added at this time. The poem was finished in 1804, as its appearance in MS M would indicate. I have given the whole poem as it appears in MS M. The poem was published in 1807. Source: MS M (see *PW*, 4:279–285, 463–465).

[I]
There was a time when meadow grove and stream
The earth and every common sight
   To me did seem
Apparrel'd in celestial light
The glory and the freshness of a dream   5
It is not now as it has been of yore
Turn wheresoe'er I may
   By night or day
The things which I have seen I see them now no more

[II]
The Rainbow comes and goes   10
And lovely is the rose
The moon doth with delight
Look round her when the heavens are bare
   Waters on a starry night
Are beautiful and fair   15
   The sunshine is a glorious birth
But yet I know wheree'er I go
That there hath pass'd away a glory from the earth

164

[III]
Now while the Birds thus sing a joyous song
   And while the young lambs bound   20
   As to the tabor's sound
To me alone there came a thought of grief
A timely utterance gave that thought relief
   And I again am strong
The cataracts blow their trumpets from the steep   25
No more shall grief of mine the season wrong
I hear the echoes through the mountains throng
The winds come to me from the fields of sleep
   And all the earth is gay
      Land and sea   30
   Give themselves up to jollity
   And with the heart of May
Doth every Beast keep holiday
   Thou Child of joy
Shout round me, let me hear thy shouts thou happy Shep-
herd boy   35

[IV]
Ye blessed Creatures I have heard the call
Ye to each other make: I see
The heavens laugh with you in your jubilee
   My heart is at your festival
   My head hath its coronal   40
Even yet more gladness I can hold it all
   O evil day if I were sullen
While the earth herself is adorning
   This sweet May morning
And the children are pulling   45
     On every side
In a thousand vallies far and wide

35 thy *del. from* [?thee]; shouts thou *interlined. Orig. reading* [?Shout
round me, let me hear thee, happy Shepherd boy]

Fresh flowers: while the sun shines warm
And the Babe leaps up in his Mother's arm
    I hear I hear with joy I hear—   50
But there's a tree of many one
A single field which I have look'd upon
Both of them speak of something that is gone
    The pansy at my feet
    Doth the same tale repeat   55
Whither is fled the visionary gleam
Where is it gone the glory and the dream

                    [V]
Our birth is but a sleep and a forgetting
The soul that rises with us our life's star
    Hath had elsewhere its setting   60
    And cometh from afar
    Not in entire forgetfulness
    And not in utter nakedness
    But trailing clouds of glory do we come
From God who is our home.   65
    Heaven lies about us in our infancy
    Shades of the prison-house begin to close
        Upon the growing Boy
    But he beholds the light and whence it flows
        He sees it in his joy   70
    The Youth who daily farther from the East
        Must travel, still is Nature's Priest
    And by the vision spendid
        Is on his way attended
At length the Man beholds it die away   75
And fade into the light of common day

                    [VI]
Earth fills her lap with pleasure of her own
Yearnings she hath in her own natural kind
And even with something of a Mother's mind
        And no unworthy aim   80

The homely nurse doth all she can
To make her foster child her Inmate Man
    Forget the glories he hath known
And that imperial palace whence he came

[VII]

Behold the Child among his new-born blisses,   85
A four year's darling of a pigmy size,
See where mid work of his own hand he lies,
Fretted by sallies of his Mother's kisses
With light upon him from his Father's eyes
    See at his feet some little plan or chart   90
Some fragment from his dream of human life
Shaped by himself with newly learned art
        A wedding or a festival
        A mourning or a funeral
And this hath now his heart   95
And unto this he frames his song
    Then will he fit his tongue
To dialogues of business love or strife
    But it will not be long
    Ere this be thrown aside   100
    And with new joy and pride
The little actor cons another part
    Filling from time to time his humourous stage
    With all the persons down to palsied age
    That Life brings with her in her Equipage   105
        As if his whole vocation
        Were endless imitation

[VIII]

O Thou whose outward seeming doth belie
        Thy Soul's immensity
Thou best philosopher who yet dost keep   110
    Thy heritage thou eye among the blind
That deaf and silent read'st the eternal deep
    Haunted for ever by the eternal mind

Thou mighty Prophet Seer blest
On whom those truth[s] do rest   115
Which we are toiling all our lives to find
    O Thou on whom thy immortality
    Broods like the day a Master o'er a Slave
    A presence which is not to be put by
    Thou unto whom the grave   120
Is but a lonely bed without the sense or sight
    Of day or the warm light
    A living place where we in waiting lie
Why with such earnest pains dost thou provoke
The years to bring the inevitable yoke   125
Thus blindly with thy blessedness at strife
Full soon thy soul shall have her earthly freight
And custom lie upon thee with a weight
Heavy as frost and deep almost as life.

        [IX]
    O joy that in our embers   130
    Is something that doth live
    That nature yet remembers
    What was so fugitive
The thought of our past years in me doth breed
Perpetual benedictions; not indeed   135
For that which is most worthy to be blest
Delight and liberty the simple creed
Of childhood whether fluttering or at rest
With new-born hope for ever in his breast,
    Not for these I raise   140
    The song of thanks and praise
But for those blank misgivings of a Creature
Moving about in worlds not realized
High instincts before which our mortal nature
Did tremble like a guilty thing surprized   145
    But for those first affections
    Those shadowy recollections
    Which be they what they may

Are yet the fountain light of all our day
Are yet the master light of all our seeing   150
    Uphold us cherish us and make
Our noisy years seem moments in the being
Of the eternal silence truths that wake
    To perish never
Which neither listlessness nor mad endeavour   155
    Nor Man nor Boy,
Nor all that is at enmity with joy
Can utterly abolish or destroy.
    Hence in a season of calm weather
    Though inland far we be   160
    Our souls have sight of that immortal sea
    Which brought us hither
Can in a moment travel thither
And see the children sport upon the shore
And hear the mighty waters rolling evermore   165
                [X]
Then sing ye Birds sing sing a joyous song
    And let the young lambs bound
    As to the Tabors sound!
We in thought will join your throng
    Ye that pipe and ye that play
    Ye that through your hearts today   170
    Feel the gladness of the May.
What though it be past the hour
Of splendour in the grass, of glory in the flower,
    We will grieve not, rather find
    Strength in what remains behind;   175
    In the soothing thoughts that spring
    Out of human suffering;
In the faith that looks through death;
In years that bring the philosophic mind
                [XI]
And Oh! ye fountains meadows field & groves   180
    Think not of any severing of our loves

Yet in my heart of hearts I feel your might
I only have relinquished one delight
To live beneath your more habitual sway;
I love the brooks that down their channels fre[t]   185
Even more than when I tripped lightly as the[y]
The innocent brightness of a new-born day
Is lovely yet
The clouds that gather round the setting sun
Do take a sober colouring from an eye   190
That hath kept watch o'er mans mortality:
Another race hath been, and other palms are w[on]
Thanks to the human heart by which we live
Thanks to its tenderness its joys and fears
To me the meanest flower that blows can give   195
Thoughts that do often lie too deep for tears.

Called "The Glow-worm" by D. W. (*DWJ*, 144); untitled in MSS
and 1807. Composed 12 April 1802 (*DWJ*, 141, 144, 147; *EY*, 1:348);
published in 1807 only. Source: W. and D. W. to C. 16 April 1802,
DCP. On the same day a copy was sent to M. H. in a letter from
D. W. to M. H., but the MS does not survive. SHP has "Mary" for
"Emma" at line 19 and a few minor variants. Presumably S. H. found
these readings in the copy made for Mary. (See *EY*, 1:348, 352; *PW*,
2:466, 541.)

Among all lovely things my Love had been,
Had noted well the stars, all flow'rs that grew
About her home, but She had never seen
A Glow-worm, never once—and this I knew.

While I was riding on a stormy night,   5
Not far from her Abode, I chanc'd to spy
A single Glowworm once; and at the sight
Down from my Horse I leapt—great joy had I.

I laid the Glowworm gently on a leaf,
And bore it with me through the stormy night   10
In my left hand—without dismay or grief
Shining, albeit with a fainter light.

When to the Dwelling of my Love I came,
I went into the Orchard quietly,
And left the Glowworm, blessing it by name,   15
Laid safely by itself, beneath a tree.

The whole next day I hop'd, and hop'd with fear:
At night the Glowworm shone beneath the tree;
I led my Emma to the place,—"Look here!"—
O joy it was for her, and joy for me!—   20

20 [O joy it was for thee, and joy *del.*] *In the letter to C. these
lines are headed* "Poem" *and a note reads* The incident of this Poem
took place about 7 years ago between Dorothy & me.

WRITTEN WHILE RESTING ON THE BRIDGE NEAR THE FOOT OF
BROTHER'S WATER, BETWEEN ONE & TWO O'CLOCK AT NOON
APRIL 16TH, 1802

The full title gives the date of composition (*EY*, 1:348) as 16 April
1802 (see *DWJ*, 144); published in 1807. Source: W. and D. W. to C.,
16 April 1802, DCP. The text of SHP differs only in accidentals. (See
EY, 1:348, 349; *PW*, 2:220, 539.)

The cock is crowing,
The stream is flowing,
The small birds twitter,
The Lake doth glitter,
The green field sleeps in the sun;   5
The Horse and his Marrow
Drag the plow and the harrow,
The cattle are grazing,
Their heads never raising,
There are forty feeding like one.   10

Like an army defeated,
The snow hath retreated,
And now doth fare ill
On the top of the bare hill;
The Plough-boy is whooping—anon—anon;   15
There's joy in the mountains,
There's life in the fountains,
Small clouds are sailing,
Blue sky prevailing;
The rain is over and gone.—   20

Title: near *del. from* at   16 *del. from* 15

Composed 18 April 1802 (*DWJ*, 146); published in 1807. Source:
SHP (see *PW*, 2:149, 150, 539).

Art thou the Bird whom man loves best
The pious Bird with scarlet breast
Our little English Robin?
The Bird that comes about our doors!
When Autumn winds are sobbing?   5
Art thou the Charles of Sweedish Boors,
Their Thomas in Finland
And Russia far Inland,
In Germany their little Hans,
The Frederick whom they love in France,   10
The Bird whom by some name or other
All men who know thee call their Brother,
The darling of Children and Men!
Could Father Adam open his eyes
And see this sight beneath the skies,   15
He'd wish to close them again.

If the Butterfly knew but his Friend,
Hither his flight he would bend,
And find his way to me
Under the branches of the Tree;   20
—In and out he darts about—
  Robin! Robin!
His little heart is throbbing:—
Can this be the Bird to man so good
That after their bewildering,   25
Did cover with leaves the little children
So painfully in the wood!—
What ails thee Robin! that thou must pursue

A beautiful creature that is gentle by nature?
Beneath the summer sky   30
From flow'r to flow'r let him fly
'Tis all that he wishes to do.

The chearer thou of our in-door sadness!
He is the friend of our summer gladness
What hinders then that ye should be   35
Playmates in the sunny weather
And fly about in the air together?
Like thy own breast
His beautiful wings in crimson are dress'd;
As if he were bone of thy bone;   40
If thou would be happy in thy nest,
O pious Bird whom man loves best
Love him, or leave him alone!

Composed in mid-April, finished 20 April 1802 (*DWJ*, 147); published in 1807. Source: SHP (see *PW*, 2:22, 23, 537).

I've watch'd you now a full half hour
Self-poized upon that yellow flower
And little Butterfly! indeed
I know not if you sleep or feed
How motionless! not frozen seas   5
More motionless, and then
What joy awaits you when the breeze
Shall find you out among the trees
And call you forth again!

This plot of orchard ground is ours   10
My trees they are, my sisters flowers
Stop here whenever you are weary
And feed as in a sanctuary
Come often to us, fear no wrong
Sit near us on the bough   15
We'll talk of sunshine and of song
And summer days when we were young
Sweet childish days that were as long
As twenty days are now.

18 *Del. from* And childish summer days as long

Perhaps composed separately but then joined as one poem, as represented here, with subhead for the second part. Composed in late April 1802 (*DWJ*, 148, 22 April 1802). D. W. notes W. "repeating the poem: 'I have thoughts that are fed by the sun'. It had been called to his mind by the dying away of the stunning of the waterfall when he came behind a stone." First published in 1944. Source: SHP (see *PW*, 2:542; 4:365, 366).

These chairs they have no words to utter
No fire is in the grate to stir or flutter
The ceiling and floor are mute as a stone
My chamber is hush'd and still
    And I am alone   5
    Happy and alone

Oh! who would be afraid of life?
    The passion the sorrow and the strife
      When he may lie
      Shelter'd so easily   10
May lie in peace on his bed
Happy as they who are dead
— — — — — — — — —

    Half an hour afterwards.
I have thoughts that are fed by the sun
    The things which I see
    Are welcome to me   15
    Welcome every one
    I do not wish to lie
    Dead, dead

13/14 *The broken line may indicate two separate poems. But S. H. similarly marks the division between the two parts of "Beggars," but with a solid line. In MS M the two parts of "These chairs" appear together marked as in SHP, but with a solid dividing line.*
16 Welcome [to me *del.*] every one

Dead without any company
   Here alone on my bed   20
With thoughts that are fed by the sun
And hopes that are welcome everyone
   Happy am I.

O life there is about thee
A deep delicious peace   25
I would not be without thee
   Stay oh stay
Yet be thou ever as now
Sweetness & breath with the quiet of death
   Peace, peace, peace.

Composed between 27 and 29 April 1802 (*DWJ*, 151, 152); published in 1897. Source: SHP (see *PW*, 2:366, 367, 542, 543).

Who leads a happy life
If its not the merry Tinker?
Not too old to have a wife
Not too much a Thinker
Through the meadows, over stiles   5
Where there are no measur'd miles
Day by day he finds his way
Among the lonely houses
Right before the Farmer's door
Down he sits his brows he knits: 10
Then his hammer he rouzes
   Batter, batter, batter
   He begins to clatter
And while the work is going on
Right good ale he bouzes   15
And when it is done away he is gone
And in his scarlet coat
With a merry note
He sings the sun to bed
And without making a pother   20
Finds some place or other
For his own careless head.

When in the woods the little Fowls
Begin their merry making
Again the jolly Tinker bowls   25
Forth with small leave taking
Through the valley up the hill

22 own *interlined*

He can't go wrong go where he will
   Tricks he has twenty
   And pastimes in plenty   30
He's the terror of Boys in the midst of their noise
When the market maiden
Bringing home her lading
Hath pass'd him in a nook
With his outlandish look   35
And visage grim & sooty
Bumming, bumming, bumming
What is that that's coming?
   Silly maid as ever was
   She thinks that she and all she has   40
   Will be the Tinker's booty
Not doubting of her dread
Like a Bullfinch black & red
The Tinker shakes his head
Laughing, laughing, laughing   45
As if he would laugh himself dead.
And thus with work or none
The Tinker lives in fun
With a light soul to cover him
And sorrow & care to blow over him   50
Whether he's up or abed.—

30 in *interlined*   38 that *del. from* this

The title is from MS M; D. W. refers to it in 1802 as "Children gathering Flowers" (*DWJ*, 151). Composed 28 April 1802 (*DWJ*, 151, 152); published in 1807. Source: SHP (see *PW*, 1:227, 228; 2:541).

That is work which I am rueing:
Do as Charles and I are doing.
Strawberry blossoms, one and all.
We must spare them—here are many:
Look at it!—the flower is small,   5
Small and low, though fair as any,
Do not touch it; summers two
I am older, Anne, than you.

Pull the primrose, Sister Anne!
Pull as many as you can.   10
Here are daisies—take your fill;
Pansies, and the cuckoo-flower;
Of the lofty daffodil
Make your bed, or make your bower;
Fill your lap and fill your bosom   15
Spare the little strawberry blossom.

Primroses the spring may love them
Summer knows but little of them;
Violets, do what you will,
Wither'd on the ground must lie   20
Daisies must be daisies still
Daisies they must live & die;
Fill your lap & fill your bosom,
Only spare the strawberry blossom!

The title is from MS M; D. W. refers to it in 1802 as "The Celandine" (*DWJ*, 153, 154). Composed 30 April and 1 May 1802 (*DWJ*, 153, 154); published in 1807. Source: MS M (see *PW*, 2:142–144).

Pansies, lilies, kingcups, daisies
Let them live upon their praises
Long as there's a sun that sets
Primroses will have their glory
Long as there are violets   5
They will have a place in story
There's a flower that shall be mine
'Tis the little Celandine

Eyes of some men travel far
For the finding of a Star   10
Up and down the heavens they go
Men that keep a mighty rout
I'm as great as they, I trow
Since the day I found the[e] out
Little flower! I'll make a stir   15
Like a great Astronomer

Modest, yet withal an elf
Bold and lavish of thyself
Since we needs must first have met
I have seen thee high and low   20
Thirty years and more, and yet
'Twas a face I did not know
Thou hast now go where I may
Fifty greetings in a day

Ere a leaf is on a bush   25
In the time before the thrush

Has a thought about its nest
Thou wilt come with half a call
Spreading out thy glossy breast
Like a careless prodigal   30
Telling tales about the sun
When we've little warmth or none

Poets, vain men in their mood
Travel with the multitude
Never heed them, I aver   35
That they all are wanton wooers
But the thrifty Cottager
Who stirs little out of doors
Joys to spy the[e] near her home
Spring is coming, thou art come   40

Comfort have thou of thy merit
Kindly unassuming spirit
Careless of thy neighbourhood
Thou dost shew thy pleasant face
On the moor and in the wood   45
In the lane—there's not a place
Howsoever mean it be
But 'tis good enough for thee

Ill befal the yellow flowers
Children of the flaring hours   50
Buttercups that will be seen
Whether we will see or no
Others too of lofty mien
They have done as worldings do
Taken praise that should be thine   55
Little humble Celandine

Prophet of delight and mirth
Scorn'd and slighted upon earth
Herald of a mighty band
Of a joyous train ensuing   60

Singing at my heart's command
In the lanes my thoughts pursuing
I will sing as doth behove
Hymns in praise of what I love

The title is from MS M; D. W. refers to it in 1802 as "The Celandine, 2nd part" (*DWJ*, 155). Composed 1 May 1802 (*DWJ*, 155); published in 1807. Source: MS M (see *PW*, 2:144–146).

Pleasures newly found are sweet
When they lie about our feet
February last my heart
First at sight of thee was glad
All unheard of as thou art   5
Thou must needs I think have had
Celandine and long ago
Praise of which I nothing know

I have not a doubt but he
Whosoe'er the man might be   10
Who the first with pointed rays
Workman worthy to be sainted
Set the sign-board in a blaze
When the risen sun he painted
Took the fancy from a glance   15
At thy glittering countenance

Soon as gentle breezes bring
News of winters vanishing
And the children build their bowers
Sticking 'kerchief-plots of mold   20
All about with full blown flowers
Thick as sheep in shepherd's fold
With the proudest thou art there
Mantling in the tiny square

Often have I sigh'd to measure   25
By myself a lonely pleasure

Sigh'd to think I read a book
Only read perhaps by me
Yet I long could overlook
Thy bright coronet and thee
And thy arch and wily ways   30
And thy store of other praise

Blythe of heart from week to week
Thou dost play at hide and seek
While the patient primrose sits   35
Like a beggar in the cold
Thou a flower of wiser wits
Slips't into thy sheltered hold
Bright as any of the train
When ye all are out again   40

Thou art not beyond the moon
But a thing beneath our shoon
Let, as old Magellen did,
Others roam about the sea
Build who will a pyramid   45
Praise it is enough for me
If there are but three or four
Who will love my little flower

The title is from SHP as well as from D. W.'s journal and is used here to distinguish it from the second version, "Resolution and Independence" (*DWJ*, 155). This first version was composed between 3 and 9 May 1802 (*DWJ*, 155, 158, 159); published in 1970 (*Cornell Library Journal*, no. 11 (Spring, 1970), pp. 59–75. Source: SHP and D. W. and W. to M. H. and S. H., 14 June 1802 (DCP). (See *PW*, 2:235–240, 539–541, 535–537; *EY*, 1:364–367.)

There was a roaring in the wind all night
The rain came heavily and fell in floods
But now the sun is rising calm and bright
The Birds are singing in the distant woods
Over his own sweet voice the stock-dove broods 5
The Jay makes answer as the magpie chatters
And all the air is fill'd with pleasant noise of waters

All things that love the sun are out of doors
The sky rejoices in the morning's birth
The grass is bright with rain drops: on the moor 10
The Hare is running races in her mirth
And with her feet she from the plashy earth
Raises a mist which glittering in the sun
Runs with her all the way wherever she doth run.

I was a Traveller upon the moor 15
I saw the hare that rac'd about with joy
I heard the woods and distant waters roar
Or heard them not, as happy as a Boy
The pleasant season did my heart employ
My old remembrances went from me wholly 20
And all the ways of men so vain & melancholy

But as it sometimes chanceth from the might
Of joy in minds that can no farther go

The title is from MS L; the poem lacks a title in all previous MSS. The revisions were made between 14 June and 5 July 1802 (*DWJ*, 175, 186, 187; *EY*, 1:364–367); published in 1807. Source: C. to Sir George Beaumont, 13 August 1803 (Coleorton Papers, MA 1581, The Pierpont Morgan Library; see *STCL*, 2:966–970; *PW*, 2:235–240). D. W. copied the poem for Coleridge on 5 July 1802, but he recopied it in his own hand for Beaumont.

There was a roaring in the wind all night;
The rain came heavily, & fell in floods;
But now the sun is rising calm and bright,
The birds are singing in the distant woods;
Over his own sweet voice the stock dove broods,   5
The jay makes answer as the magpie chatters;
And all the air is fill'd with pleasant noise of waters.

All things that love the sun are out of doors;
The sky rejoices in the morning's birth,
The grass is bright with rain-drops, on the moors   10
The hare is running races in her mirth,
And with her feet she from the plashy earth
Raises a mist, which, glittering in the sun,
Runs with her all the way wherever she doth run.

I was a Traveller then upon the Moor,   15
I saw the hare that rac'd about with joy,
I heard the woods and distant waters roar,
Or heard them not, as happy as a Boy;
The pleasant season did my heart employ,
My old remembrances went from me wholly,   20
And all the ways of men so vain and melancholy.

But, as it sometimes chanceth from the might
Of joy in minds that can no farther go,

As high as we have mounted in delight
In our dejection do we sink as low   25
To me that morning did it happen so
And fears and fancies thick upon me came
Dim sadness & blind thoughts I knew not nor could name

I heard the sky lark singing in the sky
And I bethought me of the playful hare   30
Even such a happy child of earth am I
Even as these happy creatures do I fare
Far from the world I live & from all care
But there may come another day to me
Solitude pain of heart distress & poverty.   35

My whole life I have liv'd in pleasant thought
As if life's business were a summer mood:
Who will not wade to seek a bridge or boat
How can he ever hope to cross the flood?
How can he e'er expect that others should   40
Build for him, sow for him, and at his call
Love him who for himself will take no heed at all?

I thought of Chatterton the marvelous Boy
The sleepless soul who perished in his pride
Of Him who walked in glory & in joy   45
Behind his Plough upon the mountain's side
By our own spirits we are deified
We Poets in our youth begin in gladness
But thereof comes in the end despondency and madness.

Now whether it was by peculiar grace   50
A leading from above, a something given
Yet it befel that in that lonely place
When up & down my fancy thus was driven
And I with these untoward thoughts had striven

34 there may *del. from* from another

188

As high as we have mounted in delight
In our dejection do we sink as low   25
To me that morning did it happen so;
And fears and fancies thick upon me came,
Dim sadness & blind thoughts I knew not, nor could name

I heard the sky-lark singing in the sky,
And I bethought me of the playful hare;   30
Even such a happy Child of earth am I,
Even as these happy creatures do I fare;
Far from the world I walk & from all care
But there may come another day to me;
Solitude, pain of heart, distress and poverty.   35

My whole life I have liv'd in pleasant thought
As if life's business were a summer mood,
And they who liv'd in genial faith found nought
That grew more willingly than genial good
But how can he expect that others should   40
Build for him, sow for him, and at his call
Love him who for himself will take no heed at all.

I thought of Chatterton, the marvellous Boy,
The sleepless soul who perish'd in his pride:
Of him who walk'd in glory and in joy   45
Behind his plough upon the mountain side;
By our own spirits are we deified:
We Poets in our youth begin in gladness;
But thereof comes in the end despondency & madness.

Now whether it was by peculiar grace,   50
A leading from above, a something given,
Yet it befel that in that lonely place,
When up and down my fancy thus was driven,
And I with these untoward thoughts had striven,
I spied a Man before me unawares;   55
The oldest Man he seem'd that ever wore grey hairs.

I to the borders of a Pond did come   55
By which an Old man was, far from all house or home

He seem'd like one who little saw or heard
For chimney-nook, or bed, or coffin meet
A stick was in his hand wherewith he stirr'd
The waters of the pond beneath his feet   60
Him
But
How [came he here, thought I or what can he be doing?]

He [?c]
Prov   65
But
Comi[ng together in their pilgrimage;
As if [some dire constraint of pain, or rage
Of s[ickness felt by him in times long past,]
Wh   70

He [wore a Cloak the same as women wear
As [one whose blood did needful comfort lack;
His [face look'd pale as if it had grown fair,
An[d furthermore he had upon his back
Ben[eath his Cloak a round & bulky Pack   75
A [load of wool or raiment as might seem
Bu[t on his shoulders lay as if it clave to him.]

The
B
U[pon the muddy water which he conn'd   80
A[s if he had been reading in a book

61–112 *One leaf has been torn from SHP. The lines supplied in
brackets are this editor's conjectures based upon the words or parts
of words that remain along the torn inside margins.*

63 *Supplied from MS letter (1802)*

64–70 *The words* view (*as a verb*) *and* length of time *may have appeared in this stanza (MS letter, 1802).*

My course I stopp'd as soon as I espied
The Old Man in that naked wilderness;
Close by a Pond upon the hither side
He stood alone: a minute's space, I guess,   60
I watch'd him, he continuing motionless.
To the Pool's further margin then I drew,
He all the while before me being full in view.

As a huge stone is sometimes seen to lie
Couch'd on the bald top of an eminence,   65
Wonder to all that do the same espy,
By what means it could thither come & whence;
So that it seems a thing endued with sense,
Like a Sea-beast crawl'd forth, which on a shelf
Of rock or sand reposeth, there to sun itself.   70

Such seem'd this Man, not all alive nor dead,
Nor all asleep; in his extreme old age
His body was bent double, feet and head
Coming together in their pilgrimage,
As if some dire constraint of pain, or rage,   75
Of sickness felt by him in times long past
A more than human weight upon his age had cast.

Himself he propp'd, both body, limbs and face
Upon a long grey staff of shaven wood;
And still as I drew near with gentle pace   80
Beside the little Pond or moorish flood
Motionless as a cloud the Old Man stood,
That heareth not the loud winds when they call,
And moveth altogether if it moves at all.

He wore a Cloak the same as women wear   85
As one whose blood did needful comfort lack;
His face look'd pale as if it had grown fair,

57 I espied *del. from* he espied   69 [that *del.*] crawl'd

[And now such freedom as I could I took
[And, drawing to his side, to him did say,]
"[This morning gives us promise of a glorious day."]

[A gentle answer did the Old Man make   85
[In courteous speech which forth he slowly drew;
[And him with further words I thus bespake,]
"[What kind of work is that which you pursue?
[This is a lonesome place for one like you."
[He answer'd me with pleasure & surprize,   90
[And there was while he spake a fire about his eyes.]

[His words came feeble from a feebl]e chest
[Yet each in solemn order follow'd each
[With something of a pompous utterance drest,
[Choice word & measur'd phrase, beyond the reach   95
[Of ordinary men, a stately speech,
[Such as grave livers do in Scotland use,
[Religious Men who give to God & Man their] dues.

[
[100
[
[
[
[
[   ] last   105

[   ] home:
[
[
[
[110
[
[   ] 'd

85–91 *The torn edge of the MS reveals parts of initial letters in
the conjectured stanza:* 85[?A], 86[?I], 87[?W], 90[?H], 91[?A].

And furthermore he had upon his back
Beneath his Cloak a round & bulky Pack,
A load of wool or raiment as might seem   90
That on his shoulders lay as if it clave to him

At length, himself unsettling, he the Pond
Stirr'd with his staff, & fixedly did look
Upon the muddy water which he conn'd
As if he had been reading in a book;   95
And now such freedom as I could I took
And, drawing to his side, to him did say,
"This morning gives us promise of a glorious day."

A gentle answer did the Old Man make
In courteous speech which forth he slowly drew;   100
And him with further words I thus bespake,
"What kind of work is that which you pursue?
"This is a loncsomc placc for onc likc you."
He answer'd me with pleasure & surprize,
And there was while he spake a fire about his eyes. 105

His words came feebly from a feeble chest,
Yet each [in so]lemn order follow'd each
With something of a pompous utterance drest,
Choice word & measur'd phrase, beyond the reach
Of ordinary men, a stately speech,   110
Such as grave livers do in Scotland use,
Religious Men who give to God & Man their dues.

He told me that he to the Pond had come
To gather Leeches, being old and poor,
That 'twas his calling, better far than some,   115
Though he had many hardships to endure:
From Pond to Pond he roam'd from Moor to Moor,
Housing with God's good help by choice or chance,
And in this way he gain'd an honest maintenance.

107–124 *The MS is torn where brackets occur.*

[
[
[
[
[
[
[
[115

[120
[
[
[
[   ]
I yet can gain my bread tho' in times gone   125
I twenty could have found where now I can find one

Feeble I am in health these hills to climb
Yet I procure a Living of my own
This is my summer work in winter time
I go with godly Books from Town to Town   130
Now I am seeking Leeches up & down
From house to house I go from Barn to Barn
All over Cartmell Fells & up to Blellan Tarn

With this the Old Man other matter blended
Which he deliver'd with demeanor kind   135
Yet stately in the main & when he ended
I could have laugh'd myself to scorn to find
In that decrepit man so firm a mind
God said I be my help & stay secure
I'll think of the Leech-gatherer on the lonely Moor.   140

98–126 *These four stanzas were omitted entirely when the poet*
revised.

194

The Old Man still stood talking by my side,   120
But soon his voice to me was like a stream
Scarce heard, nor word from word could I divide,
And the whole body of the Man did seem
Like one [wh]om I had met with in a dream;
Or like a Man from some far region sent   125
To give me human strength, & strong admonishment.

My former thoughts return'd, the fear that kills,
The hope that is unwilling to be fed,
Cold, pain, and labour, & all fleshly ills,
And mighty Poets in their misery dead;   130
And now, not knowing what the Old Man had said,
My question eagerly did I renew,
"How is it that you live? & what is it you do?"

He with a smile did then his words repeat
And said, that wheresoe'er they might be spied   135
He gather'd Leeches, stirring at his feet
The waters in the Ponds where they abide,
Once he could meet with them on every side;
But fewer they became from day to day,
And so his means of life before him died away.   140

While he was talking thus the lonely place,
The Old Man's shape & speech all troubl'd me;
In my mind's eye I seem'd to see him pace
About the weary Moors continually,
Wandering about alone and silently,   145
While I these thoughts within myself pursu'd,
He, having made a pause, the same discourse renew'd.

And now with this he other matter blended
Which he deliver'd with demeanor kind,
Yet stately in the main; & when he ended   150
I could have laugh'd myself to scorn to find
In that decrepit Man so firm a mind;
"God," said I, "be my help & stay secure!
"I'll think of the Leech-gatherer on the lonely Moor

Lines 6–9 of this poem were written between December 1798 and June 1800 as part of "Nutting" (see Mark L. Reed, *Wordsworth: The Chronology of the Early Years, 1770–1799* [Cambridge, Mass., 1967], pp. 331, 332); they were finally printed as part of the sequel to "Ode to Lycoris" (*PW*, 4:97, 98). But these lines appear as a freestanding poem in SHP and are referred to by D. W. on 4 May 1802 as though they made up a single poem ("'This is the spot' over and over and over again," *DWJ*, 157). Source: SHP (see *PW*, 2:543; 4:97, 98, 423, 424).

> This is the spot:—how mildly does the Sun
> Shine in between these fading leaves! the air
> In the habitual silence of this wood
> Is more than silent: and this bed of heath
> Where shall we find so sweet a resting place?   5
> Come!—let me see thee sink into a dream
> Of quiet thoughts,—protracted till thine eye
> Be calm as water, when the winds are gone
> And no one can tell whither.—My sweet Friend!
> We two have had such happy hours together   10
> That my heart melts in me to think of it.

Composed before 7 May 1802, probably around March or April, since the sparrows at Town-End were "full fledged" by 7 May (*DWJ*, 158, 159). It was published in 1807. Source: SHP. There is a transcription of this poem and "To a Butterfly" ("Stay near me") in a letter from C. to Thomas Poole, 7 May 1802 (*STCL*, 2:801), but the letter gives a later version. (See *PW*, 1:227; 2:541.)

Look! five blue eggs are gleaming there
Few visions have I seen more fair
Nor many prospects of delight
More pleasing than this simple sight.
I started seeming to espy   5
The home and little bed
The sparrow's dwelling which hard by
My Father's house in wet or dry
My Sister Dorothy and I
Together visited   10

She look'd at it as if she fear'd it
Still wishing dreading to be near it
Such heart was in her, being then
A little Prattler among men.
The blessing of my later years   15
Was with me when a Boy
She gave me eyes she gave me ears
And humble cares and delicate fears
A heart the fountain of sweet tears
And love and thought and joy.   20

6 The home *del. from* I started s (*repeating line 5*)
8 or *interlined, del. from* and   13 being *del. from* [?my sister]

[STANZAS WRITTEN IN MY POCKET COPY OF THE CASTLE OF INDOLENCE]

The title is from MS M. Composed between 9 and 11 May 1802 (*DWJ*, 159, 160) but not sent to C. until 7 June 1802 (*DWJ*, 171). Source: SHP (see *PW*, 2:25–27, 537).

Within our happy Castle there dwelt one
Whom without blame I may not overlook:
For never sun on living creature shone
Who more devout enjoyment with us took.
Here on his hours he hung as on a book;   5
On his own time he here would float away;
As doth a fly upon a summer brook:
But, go tomorrow, or belike, today,
Seek for him, he is fled; & whither none could say.

Thus often would he leave our peaceful home,   10
And find elsewhere his business or delight.
Out of our Valley's limits did he roam:
Full many a time, upon a stormy night,
His voice came to us from the neighbouring height:
Oft did we see him driving full in view   15
At mid-day, when the sun was shining bright:
What ill was on him, what he had to do,
A mighty wonder bred among our quiet crew.

Ah! piteous sight it was to see this Man,
When he came back to us a wither'd flower;   20
Or like a sinful creature pale & wan:
Down would he lie, & without strength or power
Look at the common grass from hour to hour:

Title: *W. imitates James Thomson's The Castle of Indolence in stanza form and in mood.*
1 there dwelt *del. from* dwelt there

And often times how long I fear to say,
Where apple-trees in blossom made a bower,   25
Retired in that sunshiny shade he lay,
And, like a naked Indian, slept himself away.

Great wonder to our gentle tribe it was
Whenever from our Valley he withdrew;
For happier soul no living creature has   30
Than he had, being here the long day through.
Some thought he was a lover and did woo;
Some thought far worse of him, & did him wrong
But verse was what he had been wedded to;
And his own mind did, like a tempest strong,   35
Come to him thus; and drove the weary Man along.

With him there often walked in friendly wise,
Or lay upon the moss, by brook or tree,
A noticeable Man, with large dark eyes
And a pale face, that seem'd undoubtedly   40
As if a *blooming* face it *ought* to be:
Heavy his low-hung lip did oft appear,
A face divine of heaven-born ideotcy!
Profound his forehead was, though not severe;
Yet some did think that he had little business here.   45

Ah! God forefend! his was a lawful right.
Noisy he was, and gamesome as a boy:
His limbs would toss about him with delight,
Like branches when strong winds the trees annoy.
He lack'd not implement, device, or toy,   50
To cheat away the hours that silent were:
He would have taught you how you might employ
Yourself; & many did to him repair,
And, certes, not in vain;—he had inventions rare.

Instruments had he, playthings for the ear,   55
Long blades of grass pluck'd round him as he lay;

24 fear to *del. from* [?fain wo]

These serv'd to catch the wind as it came near
Glasses he had with many colours gay;
Others that did all little things display;
The beetle with his radiance manifold,   60
A mailed angel on a battle day,
And leaves & flowers, & herbage green & gold
And all the glorious sights which fairies do behold.

He would entice that other man to hear
His music, & to view his imagery: 65
And sooth, these two did love each other dear,
As far as love in such a place could be:
There did they lie from earthly labour free,
Most happy livers as were ever seen!
If but a bird to keep them company,   70
Or butterfly sate down, they were I ween,
As pleas'd as if the same had been a maiden queen.

Composed 21 May 1802 (*DWJ*, 164); another sonnet "on Bounaparte" written at the same time has not been identified. "I grieved" was published 6 September 1802 in the *Morning Post* and in 1807. Source: SHP (see *PW*, 3:110, 111).

> I grieved for Bounaparte—with a vain
> And an unthinking grief.—The vital blood
> Of that man's mind what can it be? What food
> Fed his first hopes? What knowledge could *He* gain?
> Tis not in battles that from youth we train   5
> The Governor who must be wise & good;
> And temper with the sternness of the brain
> Thoughts motherly & meek as womanhood.
> Wisdom doth live with children round her knees:
> Books, leisure, perfect freedom, & the talk   10
> Man holds with week day man in the *hourly walk*
> Of the minds business—these are the degrees
> By which true sway doth mount; this is the stalk
> True power doth grow on, and her rights are these.

Untitled in MSS; D. W. refers to it in 1802 as the "poem on Going for Mary" and the "poem on 'Our Departure' " (*DWJ*, 166). Composed between the latter part of May and 14 June 1802 (*DWJ*, 166; *EY*, 1:365); D. W. records the poem as "finished" on 29 May 1802, but it was "altered" on 13 June. The letter to M. H. and S. H. gives the revisions (*DWJ*, 174, 175). I have printed the poem as it stands in SHP, since S. H.'s copy incorporates most of those revisions. Published in 1815. Source: SHP (see *PW*, 2:23–25, 537).

Farewell thou little Nook of mountain ground
Thou rocky corner, in the lowest stair
Of Fairfield's mighty Temple that doth bound
One side of our whole vale with grandeur rare,
Sweet Garden-orchard! of all spots that are   5
The loveliest surely man hath ever found,
Farewell! we leave thee to heaven's peaceful care
Thee and the Cottage which thou dost surround.

Our Boat is safely anchor'd by the shore;
And safely she will ride when we are gone: 10
And ye few things that lie about our door
Shall have our best protection, every one;
Fields goods and distant chattels we have none;
This is the place which holds our private store
Of things earth makes and sun doth shine upon;   15
Here are they in our sight: we have no more.

Sunshine and showers be with you, bud & bell.
For two months now in vain we shall be sought:
We leave you here in solitude to dwell
With these our latest gifts of tender thought,   20
Thou like the morning in thy saffron coat
Bright Gowan! & marsh marygold farewell

3 Of that magnificent temple which doth bound *MS letter*

Whom from the borders of the Lake we brought
And placed together near our rocky well.

We go for one to whom ye will be dear;   25
And she will love this Bower this Indian shed
Our own contrivance, building without peer:
A gentle maid! whose heart is lowly bred
Her pleasures are in wild fields gathered;
With joyousness, and with a thoughtful cheer   30
She'll come to you; to you herself will wed;
And love the blessed life which we lead here.

Dear Spot whom we have watch'd with tender heed
Bringing thee chosen plants & blossoms blown
Among the distant mountains, flower & weed   35
Which thou hast taken to thee as thy own,
Making all kindness register'd & known;
Thou for our sakes, though Nature's child indeed,
Fair in thyself and beautiful alone
Hast taken gifts which thou dost little need;   40

And, O most constant & most fickle place!
That hath a wayward heart as thou dost shew
To them who look not daily on thy face,
Who being lov'd in love no bounds dost know,
And say'st when we forsake thee "Let them go!"   45
Thou easy-hearted thing! with thy wild race
Of weeds and flowers till we return be slow
And travel with the year at a soft pace:

Help us to tell her tales of years gone by
And this sweet spring the best-beloved & best   50
Joy will be gone in its mortality,
Something must stay to tell us of the rest

33 that *SHP;* which *MS letter*
33–40 *Originally lacking but supplied in MS letter and appearing
in SHP.*
42 hath *SHP;* hast *MS letter*
48 soft *del. from* [?slow]

Here with its primroses the steep rock's breast
Glitter'd at evening like a starry sky;
And in this bush our sparrow built its nest   55
Of which I sung one song that will not die.

O happy Garden! lov'd for hours of sleep
O quiet Garden! lov'd for waking hours
For soft half slumbers that did gently steep
Our spirits carrying with them dreams of flowers 60
Belov'd for days of rest in fruit-tree bowers!
Two burning months let summer over leap
And coming back with her who will be ours
Into thy bosom we again shall creep.

53 *The rhyme was originally* primrose vest (*MS letter, and a fragment of this stanza that appears in DCP Misc.* 62).

Composed 8 June 1802 (*DWJ*, 173); published in 1807. Source: SHP
(see *PW*, 2:542; 4:9, 10).

The Sun has long been set
The stars are out by twos and threes
The little birds are piping yet
Among the bushes and the trees.
—There's the Cuckoo and one or two thrushes   5
And a noise of wind that rushes
With a noise of water that gushes:
And the cuckoo's sovereign cry
Fills all the hollow of the sky.

Who would go parading   10
In London, and masquerading,
On such a night of June
With that beautiful soft half moon;
And all these innocent blisses
On such a night as this is!—   15

[REPENTANCE]

The title is from MS L. W. states in the IF note that this poem was written at "Town-End, Grasmere. 1804"; but he then adds, "Suggested by the conversation of our next neighbor, Margaret Ashburner" (*PW*, 2:476). One such conversation was recorded by D. W. in her journal entry for 24 November 1801 (*DWJ*, 80, 81). The poem appears in SHP between two poems composed in April 1802 ("I've watch'd you now" and "Among all lovely things"). "Repentence" was no doubt among those poems composed between 12 March and 14 June 1802. The poem was published in 1820. Source: SHP (see *PW*, 2:46, 537, 538; Helen Darbishire's Appendix III to her *Poems in Two Volumes 1807*, 2d ed., rev. [Oxford, 1952], pp. 470–482, gives the correct order of the poems in SHP).

O Fools that we were we had land which we sold;
Half a dozen snug fields, fat, contented, and gay;
They'd have done us more good then another man's gold,
Could we but have been as contented as they.

When the fine Man came to us from London said I,   5
"Let him come let him come with his bags in his hand
"But Thomas be true to me Thomas we'll die
Before he shall go with an inch of the Land."

O Thomas! O Thomas! come sunshine come shower
Where's your bustle, your business, your joy & your pride   10
We could do what we would with the land, it was ours.
It lay close to the door like another fire side

And now we are strangers, go early or late;
O Thomas! like one overburthen'd with sin
Sometimes when I lift up the latch of a gate   15
I look at the fields and I cannot go in.

When I walk by the hedge on a sunshiny day
To sit in the shade of my Grandfather's Tree

Such a face it puts on I half think it will say,
What ails you that you must come creeping to me?　　20

With our pastures about us we could not be sad
Our comfort was near us if we ever were cross'd
But Thomas we sold the best Friend that we had
And little we knew what a Friend we had lost.

When my sick crazy body had lain without sleep,　　25
What a comfort at sunrise it was when I stood
And look'd down on the fields and the Cows & the Sheep
From the top of the hill, 'twas like youth in my blood

Now I sit in the house and am dull as a snail
And often I hear the Church bell with a sigh　　30
When I think to myself, "we've no land in the vale,
Save six feet of earth where our Forefathers lie."

19 will *interlined, del. from* would　　27 on *interlined*

Composed probably in May 1802 (see lines 1 and 14 of the poem and D. W.'s description of Bullfinches on 28 May 1802, *DWJ*, 165, 166). Mark Reed has suggested a date between 16 April and 8 July 1802 (that is, between the return from Eusemere and the day before the early departure for Gallow Hill). Source: MS M (see *PW*, 2:139–141). W. in the IF note dates it "1803," but links it with the Daisy poems which were composed in 1802 (*PW*, 2:490, 491).

The May is come again: how sweet
To sit upon my Orchard-seat,
And Birds and Flowers once more to greet
   My last years Friends together,
My thoughts they all by turns employ,   5
A whispering leaf is now my joy:
And then, a bird will be the toy,
   That doth my fancy tether.

One have I mark'd the happiest guest
In all this covert of the blest.   10
Hail to thee far above the rest
   In joy of voice and pinion!
Thou Linnet, in thy green array,
Presiding spirit here to day,
Dost lead the revels of the May,   15
   And this is thy dominion.

While Birds and Butterflies and Flowers
Make all one band of paramours,
Thou, ranging up and down the Bowers,
   Art sole in thy employment: 20
A Life, a Presence like the air,
Scattering thy gladness without care,
Too blessed with any one to pair,
   Thyself thy own enjoyment.

Upon yon tuft of hazel trees   25
That twinkle to the gusty breeze
Behold him, perch'd in ecstasies,
    Yet seeming still to hover,
There while the flutter of his wings
Upon his back and body flings   30
Shadows and sunny glimmerings
    That cover him all over!

While thus before my eyes he gleams
A Brother of the leaves he seems
When in a moment forth he teems   35
    His little song in gushes;
As if it pleas'd him to disdain
And mock the form which he did feign,
While he was dancing with the train
    Of Leaves among the bushes.   40

27 Behold *del. from illeg. word*

Perhaps, like "The Green Linnet," the three Daisy poems—"In youth," "With little here," and "Bright Flower"—were composed between 16 April and 8 July. In a note to the 1807 *Poems*, W. says he wrote these poems in 1802 (*PW*, 2:490). The source for "In youth" is MS M (see *PW*, 2:135–138). That for the other two poems is MS L (see *PW*, 2:138, 139; 4:67, 68).

In youth from rock to rock I went
From hill to hill in discontent
Of pleasure high and turbulent
    Most pleas'd when most uneasy
But now my own delights I make   5
My thirst at every rill can slake
And gladly nature's love partake
    Of thee sweet daisy

Whene'er a milder day appears
Thee Winter in the garland wears   10
That thinly shades his few grey hairs
    Spring cannot shun thee
Whole Summer fields are thine by right
And Autumn melancholy Wight
Doth in thy crimson head delight   15
    When rains are on thee

In shoals and bands a Morrice train
Thou greet'st the Traveller in the lane
If welcome once thou count'st it gain,
    Thou art not daunted,   20
Nor cars't if thou be set at naught:
And oft alone in nooks remote
We meet thee like a pleasant thought
    When such are wanted

I saw the[e] glittering from afar   25
And here thou art a pretty Star
Not quite so fair as many are
    In heaven above thee
Yet like a star with glittering breast
Self-pois'd in air thou seem'st to rest   30
May peace come never to his nest
    Who shall reprove thee

Be violets in their secret mews
The flowers the wanton zephers chuse
Proud be the rose with rain and dews   35
    Her head impearling!
Thou livs't to follow humbler aims
Yet shall not want thy tender names:
Thou art indeed by many claims
    The Poets darling.   40

If to a rock from rains He fly
Or some bright day of April sky
Imprison'd by the sun He lie
    Near the green holly
And wearily at length should fare;   45
He need but look about, and there
Thou art! a Friend at hand to scare
    His melancholy!

A thousand times in rock or bower
Ere thus I have lain couch'd an hour   50
Have I deriv'd from thy sweet power
    Some apprehension
Some steady love some chance delight
Some memory that had taken flight
Some chime of fancy wrong or right   55
    Or stray invention

41 from *del. from* in   47 Scare *del. from* [?share]
55 chime *del. from* [?shape]

When stately passions in me burn
If some chance look to thee should turn
I drink out of an humbler urn
    A lowlier pleasure   60
A homely sympathy that heeds
The common life our nature breeds
A wisdom fitted to the needs
    Of hearts at leisure

And more than all I number yet   65
The whole year long another debt
Which I to thee wherever met
    Am daily owing
An instinct, call it a blind sense,
A happy genial influence,   70
Coming one knows not how nor whence,
    Nor whither going.

Child of the year that round dost run
Thy course, bold Lover of the sun
And jocund when the day's begun   75
    As morning Leveret
Thou long the Poet's praise shalt gain;
Thou wilt be more belov'd by men
In times to come: thou not in vain
    Art nature's favorite.   80

The headnote for the first Daisy poem, above, supplies the information about this one.

With little here to do or see
Of things that in the great world be,
Sweet Daisy! oft I talk to thee,
    For thou art worthy,
Thou unassuming Common-place   5
Of Nature, with that homely face,
And yet with something like a grace,
    Which Love makes for thee!

Oft do I sit by thee at ease,
And weave a web of similies,   10
Loose types of Things through all degrees,
    Thoughts of thy raising;
And many a fond and idle name
I give to thee, for praise or blame,
As is the humour of the game,   15
    While I am gazing.

A Nun demure of lowly port,
Or sprightly Maiden of Love's Court,
In thy simplicity the sport
    Of all temptations;   20
A Queen in crown of rubies drest,
A Starvling in a scanty vest,
Are all, as seem to suit thee best,
    Thy appellations.

A little Cyclops, with one eye   25
Staring to threaten and defy,
That thought comes next—& instantly

The freak is over,
The Shape will vanish, and behold!
A silver Shield with boss of gold,   30
That spreads itself, some Fairy bold
   In fight to cover.

I see thee glittering from afar
And then thou art a pretty Star,
Not quite so fair as many are   35
   In heaven above thee!
Yet like a Star, with glittering crest,
Self poised in air thou seems't to rest;—
May Peace come never to his nest,
   Who shall reprove thee.   40

Sweet Flower! for by that name at last,
When all my reveries are past,
I call thee, and to that cleave fast,
   Sweet silent Creature!
That breath'st with me in sun and air,   45
Do thou, as thou art wont, repair
My heart with gladness, and a share
   Of thy meek nature!

25–32 *Inserted at time of preparing copy for printer; sewn over the
sheet in MS L.*

33–40 *Compare lines* 25–30 *from* "In youth." *W. transferred the
lines to this poem in 1806–1807.*

42 reveries *reinstated*

The headnote for the first Daisy poem, above, supplies the information about this one.

Bright Flower, whose home is every where!
A Pilgrim bold in Nature's care,
And all the long year through the heir
    Of joy or sorrow,
Methinks that there abides in thee   5
Some concord with humanity,
Given to no other flower I see
    The forest throrough!

Is it that Man is soon deprest?
A thoughtless Thing! who, once unblest,   10
Does little on his memory rest
    Or on his reason,
And Thou would'st teach him how to find
A shelter under every wind,
A hope for times that are unkind   15
    And every season?

Thou wander'st the wide world about,
Uncheck'd by pride or scrupulous doubt,
With friends to greet thee, or without,
    Yet pleased & willing;   20
Meek, yielding to the occasion's call,
And all things suffering from all,
Thy function apostolical
    In peace fulfilling.

3 heir *del. from illeg. word*   4 or *interlined, del. from* and
8 throrough *so MS*

Probably composed in the spring of 1802; its appearance in SHP
is strong evidence for this date (see *PW*, 2:491, for de Selincourt's dating). Published in 1807. Source: SHP (see *PW*, 2:141, 142, 538, 539).

Up with me, up with me into the clouds!
For thy song, Lark! is strong
Up with me up with me into the clouds!
   Singing, singing
With all the clouds about us ringing,   5
   We two will sail along.

I have sung in wildernesses dreary;
But today my heart is weary
Had I now the soul of a Fairy
Up to thee would I fly.   10

There is madness about thee and joy divine
In that song of thine:
Up with me up with me powerfully
I will yoke myself to thee
And we'll travel merrily;   15
Up with me, up with me high & high
To thy banquetting place in the sky.
   Joyous as morning
   Thou art laughing & scorning
   Thou hast a nest which thou lov'st best;   20
And though little troubled with sloth,
Drunken Lark! thou wouldst be loth
To be such a traveller as I.

Happy happy Liver,
   With a soul as strong as a mountain river   25
   Pouring out praise to th'almighty giver,

Joy and jollity be with us both!
Hearing thee or else some other
As merry a brother,
I on earth will go plodding on   30
By myself chearfully till the day is done.

Composed between late April and June 1802; see Jonathan Wordsworth, "The New Wordsworth Poem," *College English*, 27(1966):455–
465, and Mark L. Reed, "More on the Wordsworth Poem," *College
English*, 28(1967):60–61. First published in the *New Statesman*, 31 July
1964. Source: The poem appears in a letter from Charles A. Elton to
Mrs. Julia Hallam, 22 September 1807.

Late on a breezy vernal eve
   When breezes wheel'd their whirling flight;
I wander'd forth; and I believe
   I never saw so sweet a sight.

It nodded in the breeze   5
   It rustled in mine ear;
Fairest of blossom'd trees
   In hill or valley, far or near:

No tree that grew in hill or vale
   Such blithesome blossoms e'er display'd: 10
They laugh'd and danc'd upon the gale;
   They seem'd as they could never fade:
As they could never fade they seem'd;
   And still they danc'd, now high, now low;
In very joy their colours gleam'd: 15
   But whether it be thus or no;
That while they danc'd upon the wind
They felt a joy like humankind:
That this blithe breeze which cheerly sung
While the merry boughs he swung;   20
Did in that moment, while the bough
   Whisper'd to his gladsome singing:
Feel the pleasures that ev'n now
   In my breast are springing:

And whether, as I said before,   25
    These golden blossoms dancing high,
    These breezes piping thro' the sky
Have in themselves of joy a store:
And mingling breath and murmur'd motion
Like eddies of the gusty ocean,   30
Do in their leafy morris bear
Mirth and gladness thro the air:
As up and down the branches toss,
And above and beneath and across
The breezes brush on lusty pinion   35
Sportive struggling for dominion:
If living sympathy be theirs
    And leaves and airs,
The piping breeze and dancing tree
Are all alive and glad as we: 40
Whether this be truth or no
I cannot tell, I do not know;
Nay—whether now I reason well,
I do not know, I cannot tell.
But this I know, and will declare,   45
    Rightly and surely *this* I know;
That never here, that never there,
    Around me, aloft, or alow;
Nor here nor there, nor anywhere
Saw I a scene so very fair.   50
And on this food of thought I fed
Till moments, minutes, hours had fled:
And had not sudden the church-chimes
    Rung out the well-known peal I love;
I had forgotten Peter Grimes,   55
    His nuts and cyder in the apple-grove:
I say, and I aver it true,
    That had I not the warning heard
        Which told how late it grew:
(And I to Grimes had pledg'd my word;)   60

In that most happy mood of mind
　　There like a Statue had I stood, till now:
　　　And when my trance was ended
　　　And on my way I tended,
　　Still, so it was, I know not how,　　　　　　　　　　65
But pass'd it not away, that piping wind:
For as I went, in sober sooth
　　It seem'd to go along with me;
I tell you now the very truth,
　　It seem'd part of myself to be:　　　　　　　　　　70
That in my inner self I had
Those whispering sounds which made me glad.
　　Now if you feel a wish dear Jones!
　　　To see these branches dancing so;
　　Lest you in vain should stir your bones,　　　　　　75
　　　I will advise you when to go:
　　That is, if you should wish to see
　　This piping, skipping Barberry:
　　(For so they call the shrub I mean,
　　Whose blossom'd branches thus are seen,　　　　　80
　　　Uptossing their leafy shrouds
　　　　As if they were fain to spring
　　　　On the whirl-zephyr's wing,
　　　　　Up to the clouds.)
　　If Jacob Jones, you have at heart　　　　　　　　85
　　　To hear this sound and see this sight:
[Then this] advise I do impart,
　　[That] Jacob you don't go by night;
　　[　　　　　] possible the shrub so green
　　[　　　　　] low, may not well be seen:　　　　90
[Nor Jaco]b, would I have you go
When the blithe winds forbear to blow;
I think it may be safely then averr'd
　　The piping leaves will not be heard.

86–91 *Part of the last page has been torn away with the seal. The*
conjectures are Jonathan Wordsworth's.

But when the wind rushes   95
    Thro brakes and thro bushes;
And around, and within, and without,
    Makes a roar and a rout;
        Then may you see
        The Barberry-tree;   100
        With all its yellow flow'rs
        And interwoven bow'rs:
        Toss in merry madness
        Ev'ry bough of gladness:
And dance to and fro to the loud-singing breeze,   105
The blithest of gales, and the maddest of trees:
        And then like me
    Ev'n from the blossoms of the Barberry,
    Mayst thou a store of thought lay by
For present time and long futurity: 110
    And teach to fellow-men a lore
        They never learn'd before;
    The manly strain of nat'ral poesy.

W. dated "The Affliction of Mary _____ of _____" and "The Forsaken" 1804. The origin of "The Forsaken" is explained in the IF
note as an "overflow" from "The Affliction of Mary" (later "Margaret,"
1820; see *PW*, 2:473, 476). However, as de Selincourt points out, "The
Affliction" appears in MS L with some introductory lines and the nota-
tion "Written for the Lyrical Ballads." De Selincourt rejects 1802 as a
possible date because "no additions [to *Lyrical Ballads*, 3d ed., 1802]
were made" (*PW*, 2:473). But early in March of 1802, W. wrote two
new stanzas for "Ruth" which did appear in 1802 (*DWJ*, 128), and
shortly thereafter he wrote "The Sailor's Mother," "Alice Fell," and
"Beggars," all poems in the mode of *Lyrical Ballads*. It seems reasonable to suppose then that "The Affliction" and "The Forsaken"
were written sometime after the taking up of "Ruth" (4 to 7 March,
DWJ, 126–129) and before the publication of the third edition in
April of 1802 (*EY*, 1:345, 346, D. W. to R. W., 6 April 1802). "The
Affliction of Mary" was published in 1807, "The Forsaken" in 1842.
Source: "The Affliction," MS L (see *PW*, 2:47–50); "The Forsaken,"
DCP Verse 92 (1836–1847; see *PW*, 2:32).

Where art thou, my beloved Son,
Where art thou, worse to me than dead?
Oh find me, prosperous or undone!
Or, if the grave be now thy bed,
Why am I ignorant of the same   5
That I may rest; and neither blame,
Nor sorrow may attend thy name?

Seven years, alas, to have received
No tidings of an only Child;
To have despair'd, and have believ'd,   10
And be for evermore beguil'd!
Sometimes with thoughts of very bliss;

10 despair'd *del. from* despaired

I catch at them, and then I miss;
Was ever darkness like to this?

He was among the prime in worth,   15
An object beauteous to behold;
Well born, well bred; I sent him forth
Ingenuous, innocent, and bold:
If things ensued that wanted grace
As hath been said, they were not base;   20
And never blush was on my face.

Ah! little doth the Young One dream,
When full of play and childish cares,
What power hath even his wildest scream,
Heard by his Mother unawares!   25
He knows it not, he cannot guess:
Years to a Mother bring distress;
But do not make her love the less.

Neglect me! no I suffer'd long
From that ill thought; and being blind,   30
Said, Pride shall help me in my wrong;
Kind Mother have I been, as kind
As ever breathed: and that is true;
I've wet my path with tears like dew,
Weeping for him when no one knew.   35

My Son, if thou be humbled, poor,
Hopeless of honour and of gain,
Oh! do not dread thy Mother's door;
Think not of me with grief and pain:
I now can see with better eyes;   40
And worldly grandeur I despise,
And fortune with her gifts and lies.

Alas! the fowls of Heaven have wings,
And blasts of Heaven will aid their flight;
They mount, how short a voyage brings   45

The Wanderers back to their delight!
Chains tie us down by land and sea;
And wishes, vain as mine, may be
All that is left to comfort thee.

Perhaps some dungeon hears thee groan,   50
Maim'd, mangled by inhuman men;
Or Thou upon a Desart thrown
Inheritest the Lion's Den;
Or hast been summoned to the Deep,
Thou, Thou and all thy mates, to keep   55
An incommunicable sleep.

I look for Ghosts; but none will force
Their way to me; 'tis falsely said
That there was ever intercourse
Betwixt the living and the dead;   60
For, surely, then I should have sight
Of him I wait for day and night,
With love and longings infinite.

My apprehensions come in crowds;
I dread the rustling of the grass;   65
The very shadows of the clouds
Have power to shake me as they pass:
I question things, and do not find
One that will answer to my mind;
And all the world appears unkind.   70

Beyond participation lie
My troubles, and beyond relief:

46 [again *del.*] to their delight!
55 Thou, Thou and all *del. from*
   Thou, Thou, all all *del. from*
   Thou, Thou, thou
67 they *interlined, del. from* I   71 lie *del. from* he

If any chance to heave a sigh
They pity me, and not my grief.
Then come to me, my Son, or send
Some tidings that my woes may end;
I have no other earthly friend.

The peace which others seek they find
The heaviest storms not longest last
Heaven grants even to the guilty mind
An amnesty for what is past
When will my sentence be reversed   5
I only pray to know the worst
And wish as if my heart would burst

Ofttimes it seems that silent years
Bring an unquestionable tale
And yet they leave it short, & fears   10
And hopes are strong & will prevail
My calmest faith escapes not pain
And feeling that the hope is vain
I think that he will come again.

2 The *del. to* Their   8 Ofttimes it seems *del. to* O weary struggle!
9 *Del. to* Tell seemingly no doubtful tale
13 *DCP Verse 102 reads* hopes are vain

This poem, perhaps by D. W., corresponds with the phrasing of *DWJ*, 148, 22 April 1802. It appears only in MS M and was first published by de Selincourt in 1947 (*PW*, 4:365).

I have been here in the Moon-light
I have been here in the Day
I have been here in the Dark Night
And the Stream was still roaring away

*Wordsworth's Experiments
with Tradition*

Designed by R. E. Rosenbaum.
Composed by Vail-Ballou Press, Inc.,
in 11 point linotype Baskerville, 2 points leaded,
with display lines in Baskerville monotype 353.
Printed letterpress from type by Vail-Ballou Press,
on Glatfelter Offset Vellum, 60 pound basis.
Bound by Vail-Ballou Press
in Interlaken ALA book cloth
and stamped in All Purpose gold foil.